# GALVESTON'S
# TREMONT
# HOUSE HOTEL

# GALVESTON'S
# TREMONT
# HOUSE HOTEL

*• A History •*

KATHLEEN SHANAHAN MACA

THE
History
PRESS

Published by The History Press
Charleston, SC
www.historypress.com

The second Tremont House Hotel in Galveston, as it appeared in 1925. *Photo courtesy of the Galveston Texas History Center of Rosenberg Library, Galveston, Texas.*

First published 2024

Manufactured in the United States

ISBN 9781467152266

Library of Congress Control Number: 2024931513

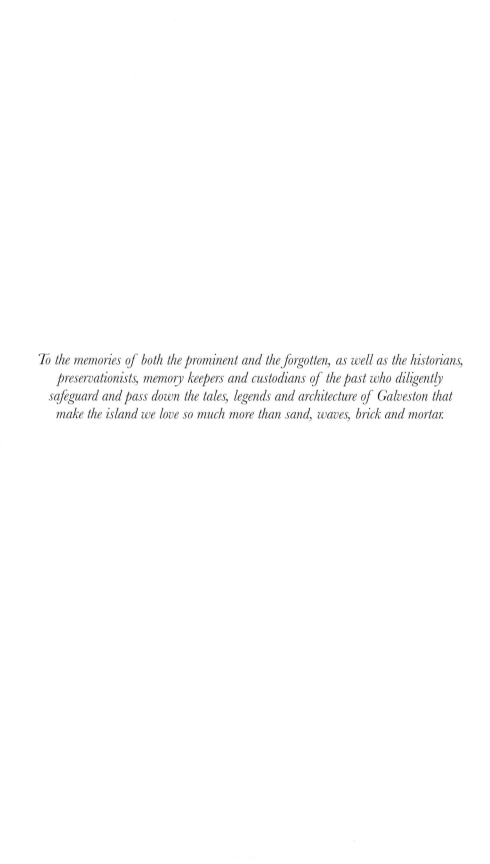

*To the memories of both the prominent and the forgotten, as well as the historians, preservationists, memory keepers and custodians of the past who diligently safeguard and pass down the tales, legends and architecture of Galveston that make the island we love so much more than sand, waves, brick and mortar.*

# CONTENTS

Acknowledgements                                          9
Introduction                                             11

PART I: GALVESTON'S FIRST TREMONT HOUSE
  1. 1839 Tremont House                        15
  2. Sam Houston's Plea                        22
  3. Fire of 1865                              25

PART II: PRIDE OF GALVESTON
  4. A New Plan                                 29
  5. Envy of the South                         31
  6. Grand Initial Ball                        39
  7. Architect Nicholas J. Clayton            42
  8. Tremont Years 1877–1928                   45
  9. Showman Buffalo Bill Cody                 58
  10. 1880 Mardi Gras                          64
  11. President Ulysses S. Grant               67
  12. Actor Edwin Booth                        76
  13. 1885 Explosion                           79
  14. Author Stephen Crane                     84
  15. A Floating Coffin                        88
  16. 1900 Storm                               92
  17. Angel in the Aftermath                   99

18. The Fisher Sisters                                    105
19. The Missing Manager                                   109
20. Closing the Register                                  113

PART III: A NEW BEGINNING
21. Blum Building                                         121
22. Architect Eugene T. Heiner                            125
23. The Merchant Prince                                   128
24. Mistrots and Newspapermen                             132
25. McDonnell Building                                    135
26. George and Cynthia Woods Mitchell                     146
27. Tremont House: A Rebirth                              151
28. Toujouse Bar                                          164
29. Hotel Hauntings                                       169
30. Mardi Gras Arches                                     173

Index                                                     181
About the Author                                          187

# ACKNOWLEDGEMENTS

S pecial thanks to Sean McConnell at the Galveston Texas History Center, Jeff Ossenkop and Jordyn Cowan of The Tremont House, Michael Gaertner and Jodi Wright-Gidley of the Galveston County Museum, along with family and friends who provided encouragement throughout the research process of this project.

# INTRODUCTION

Welcome to The Tremont House in Galveston, Texas—a stately edifice with a history that spans over 185 years.

Since before Texas was a state, visitors have sought shelter at one of the incarnations of the hotel, which has played host to famous historical figures, celebrities, soldiers, international dignitaries, locals and visitors from around the world.

Alternately referred to as both The Tremont House and Tremont Hotel through the years, the hotels have witnessed nearly every significant event that has ever taken place on the island. They have offered refuge through the Civil War, Spanish-American War, World Wars I and II, hurricanes and more and a place of retreat and celebration during happier times.

If you ask Galvestonians how many Tremont Houses have graced the island, the common answer is "three." And that is true, to a point. Three separate hotels have been built as Tremont House since the 1830s. But in between the existence of those three, at least two other hotels adopted the name for their own use.

The first Tremont House, a wood frame building, was built in 1839. After it was lost to fire in 1865, an inn owned by Mayor Charles H. Leonard adopted the name—and perhaps the fate—or his establishment on Church Street. It may have been karma that caused Leonard's hotel, along with his own home next door, to burn to the ground three years later.

The most famous of the earlier Tremont Houses, much grander than any before it, opened in 1877 and for half a century became a coveted destination for travelers from around the world. It witnessed the most elegant era of the island and all those who created and experienced it.

Several years after the loss of that exquisite establishment, the name was adopted again by a small hotel for a short time. Ironically, the location of that inn is now incorporated into the present-day Tremont House, which opened in 1985.

Today's Tremont House is creating its own chapter in the long history of these hotels while honoring their legacy.

The stories that took place within the walls of these hotels rival any novel, and the cast of characters who lived them outshines any movie. This book invites you to check into the past and explore the colorful tales of Galveston's Tremont Houses.

# Part I

---*---

# GALVESTON'S FIRST TREMONT HOUSE

# 1

# 1839 TREMONT HOUSE

The first Tremont House stood on the southwest corner of Tremont and Postoffice Streets and was owned by prominent Baltimore businessman Henry Howell Williams and a handful of associates. The firm of McKinney & Williams began construction in 1837 and had the wooden framework erected, but it was left in shambles by a gale that swept across the island during the first week of October. Known as Racer's Hurricane, after a British naval ship that it damaged, it was the most devastating local weather event recorded up to that date.

Construction began once again, and the Tremont opened its doors on April 3, 1839. Nathaniel Norwood leased the hotel and became its first proprietor.

A square wooden two-story building that one Austin newspaper described as "sturdy and stout," the Tremont had long, impressive galleries of about forty feet on both floors spanning the length of the north and east façades.

The ground floor featured a bar and a large billiard saloon. Suites of rooms sat above the expansive one-hundred-by-fifty-foot dining room. It made headlines across the country as the largest and most tastefully furnished hotel in Texas.

The official grand opening was celebrated on April 21, 1839, with a ball to commemorate the anniversary of the Battle of San Jacinto. Tickets to the event cost fifty dollars in Texas currency or twenty-five in coins. The difference in price reflected the unstable status of the Republic of Texas at the time.

Attendees from Houston and surrounding counties came to enjoy the music, supper and the company of other prominent citizens. Accounts of the day note that the choicest wines, confections and fruits to be had from New Orleans were procured for the occasion.

Later that year, a colonial secretary under the governor of the Windward Islands named Francis C. Sheridan was sent to Texas. His assignment was to observe and report his experiences back to England, to contribute to deliberations then going on in London of whether to formally recognize the new republic. He filled his journal with detailed descriptions, down to smells and tastes, of Galveston and his stay at the Tremont House.

He began his account by relating that he was greeted at the port and taken to "The" hotel to be introduced to Norwood, who extended a gracious welcome and promised him accommodations. But the proprietor first insisted they have a drink at the bar, where the visitor noted the surroundings as being much like any bar in England, with a counter, glasses, liquors and cigars in tumblers.

What fascinated the visitor about the bar was that it served as a "club" by night, but during the day, tradesmen, merchants and ship captains met to drum up business in the same room. He described a spread of cold meats, pickles, bread and butter and more that was generously laid out on the bar at noon for anyone who purchased a drink.

"At the close of the day," he noted most likely with a bit of dismay, "the room was generally crammed, and the time [was] spent in talking and spitting."

Sheridan's journal describes the method in which meals were served with an obvious tone of alarm concerning the lack of manners among the rough-edged Texans.

"The regulation attending the feeding at the Tremont House—such was the aristocratic name of the Galveston Hotel—are strictly American. At the eighth hour in the morning—Dingle, Dingle, Dingle, goes a bell of the… parlour at which magic sound the doors of a large room which runs the whole length of the building are thrown open and the crowds of boarders which had been gradually accumulating rush head-long in, and in less than ten minutes rush head-long out again."

After guests were served, the proprietor and his family ate their meal in the dining room, followed by the cook and other staff.

"Dinner is conducted on precisely similar principles at 3 p.m.," he continued in amazement, "thus reversing the British mode of feeding, three relays of guests being apportioned to one course instead of three courses to one relay of guests."

"An ample supper concludes the day and having spit, chewed, drank and smoked until 10:30 or 11:00 p.m., beds are sought and in a brief space the moon is gazing on no quieter place than Galveston."

The sleeping arrangements offered another surprise to the British traveler, who was led to a room he portrayed as being "about 15 feet by 10 feet with six beds for as many gentlemen, with two small basins with jugs to correspond, and a roaring stove fire in the center of the room."

Though putting multiple guests in one room sounds odd by today's standards, it wasn't uncommon at the time to accommodate single guests of the same gender together.

The next morning, frustrated by trying to shave in a cracked mirror, he ventured out to find a local barber.

The trip was not entirely unpleasant, and a grand ball given at the Tremont in his honor made quite an impression on Sheridan, who commented on the tasteful decorations and the "good number of well-dressed and pretty women" in attendance.

The dining room was transformed into a dancing area with flags of England, the United States, Texas and France hanging from the walls. During the festivities, he was introduced to Sam Houston, whom he described as a "very gentleman-like fine looking old general." The music and dancing lasted into the morning hours.

The 1839 holiday season graced Tremont House with the first of a series of Yuletide balls that would become a community tradition. Grand balls and dinners that celebrated the anniversary of victory at San Jacinto, Christmas, New Year's Eve and the Fourth of July became annual occasions at the hotel.

As time passed and the reputation of the Tremont grew, accommodations improved. A three-story brick addition that extended eighty feet along Tremont Street to the alley was built and connected with the wooden buildings by a covered bridge.

Most likely a reflection of the republic's economy, Norwood announced in 1841 that the Tremont would no longer accept credit for payment for lodging or bar bills. Later that year, he left to become proprietor of the Houston House in Houston.

In its prime, the Tremont was the scene of many important affairs and rivaled the best hotels in the country. It hosted innumerable important political and business figures of the day from America and Europe.

General Sam Houston used the hotel as his headquarters whenever he was in Galveston, and there are letters written from the Tremont to his wife, Margaret Lea Houston, in the Sam Houston archives. She also stayed at the hotel multiple times, whenever the couple needed access to the port or visited friends on the island.

Other guests included General Memucan Hunt Jr., the Texan minister in Washington; Anson Jones, the last president of the Republic of Texas; Commander Robert Field of the U.S. Navy; and Charles A. Wickliffe, commissioner to Texas from the United States. The ministers of France and England stayed there, and Prince Carl of Solms-Braunfels resided there for a short time before making plans for a castle (never realized) in what became New Braunfels, Texas.

The first public dinner at the old Tremont was given in honor of General J. Pinckney Henderson, minister to France from the Republic of Texas, and was presided over by the Honorable John M. Allen, mayor of the city. Toasts and speeches made by attendees, said to have been "not large—no more than one hundred people," were eagerly read about in the next day's newspapers by those not in attendance.

Other dinners were held in honor of Anson Jones, Moses Austin Bryan and other notable citizens.

Acting as a large community house, citizens conducted meetings and business there, registered to vote and utilized the dining room as a polling place during elections.

Trinity Episcopal Church had recently completed construction of its new sanctuary when, on September 17 and 18, 1842, a tropical storm struck the island. The church, which had been elevated on wooden blocks several feet from the ground, was washed from its supports and damaged by the four-foot storm surge.

Less than one week later, a meeting was held at Tremont House among members of the community to plan how to finance repairs to the church since the congregation's accounts had been exhausted in the original construction. A fundraising drive was begun that day.

An advertisement in the *Galveston Daily News* on November 25, 1843, touted, "The well-known house Tremont House is now in first-rate order for the reception of boarders. The table will always be supplied with the best the market affords; and the subscriber pledges himself that no pains shall be spared to make his friends comfortable. Rates of board at this house are reduced from two dollars to $1.50 per day, and nine dollars per week."

On Christmas 1845, what some locals considered the last Christmas of the Republic of Texas, Tremont House hosted a large gathering of people who were determined to spend the day in style. One attendee noted that the event was crowded by several generals, colonels, majors and a number of captains. Another informed the stranger not to take the titles too seriously, as many of them were honorary.

In 1846, after the fall of Monterrey in the Mexican-American War, many Texan soldiers were welcomed home by a grand banquet at the Tremont House. Described by witnesses as a gloriously elaborate experience, it was unusual in that it was held for the private soldiers as well as the officers.

During the winter of 1848–49, a young lawyer named Rutherford B. Hayes, who would later become president of the United States, made a horseback riding trip through Texas. Hayes, his uncle and Eliza Perry rode a stage through San Luis to reach Galveston Island, reaching Tremont House at about midnight. During their three-day stay, he recorded activities in his diaries such as riding horses on the beach. He never forgot his trip to Texas and referred to the Tremont as a "grand hotel."

In the era of the first Galveston Tremont, hotels served as boardinghouses as well as accommodations for travelers. Among the permanent residents listed at the hotel in the April 1850 census were the proprietor Joshua Clark Shaw; his wife, Lucy; their three children; and a female servant. Additional residents included J.P. Collins, a clerk at the hotel; John R. Lyons, the hotel's barkeeper, and his wife, Julia; sixteen-year-old William Cotton, the bar assistant; and a list of others including a livery stable keeper, several attorneys, a physician, merchants and a gentleman from Maine with his young family.

To keep up with the growing number of hotels in the area, the Tremont was remodeled and refitted with updates in 1856. After it reopened, the *Houston Telegraph* declared, "We have several good hotels in Houston, but none on anything like the scale of the Tremont."

Among the first to enjoy the renovations were the Washington Guards, who held their third Anniversary Ball at the hotel on February 22, 1857, inviting the Houston Chapter of the Guards to attend. In order to ensure a successful event, they also extended invitations to ladies from Houston and surrounding towns "so that we may expect the occasion to be graced by a very large and brilliant display."

Rates of services at the Tremont in May 1857 were posted in the newspaper as follows:

| | |
|---|---|
| *Board and lodging per day* | *$2.00* |
| *Children and servants* | *$1.00* |
| *Breakfast* | *$0.50* |
| *Dinner* | *$0.75* |

| | |
|---|---|
| *Supper* | *$0.50* |
| *Lodging* | *$0.75* |
| *Day boarders per month* | *$25.00* |

*Permanent board and lodging according to the room occupied.*

Though the rates were in line with other hotels and the Tremont House was still considered the best Galveston had to offer, business dwindled during the summer off-seasons, and maintaining the hotel was difficult.

In July 1857, notices began appearing in local papers offering the property for lease or sale and continued through the spring of the following year. Once a hub of community activity, the Tremont sat empty.

The partnership of Ayers & Jacobs finally leased the neglected structure in March 1858 and decorated it with new furnishings for a grand reopening the following month, much to the community's delight.

From the time the hotel was constructed, Tremont Street was challenging to travel. Initially marshy, it was later filled (both purposely and by winds) with a deep layer of sand. The rocky sand made travel from downtown to the beach difficult for horses and carriages.

A meeting was held at Tremont House by city officials in August 1858 to remedy the issue by laying down an oyster shell road the entire length of Tremont Street, extending all the way to the beach. The $2,000 project turned Tremont into the most favorable road in town for commerce and pleasure for visitors and residents.

Pranksters made sure the New Year's Eve Party that took place at the Tremont to welcome in the year 1859 was especially memorable. A jovial Texas cattleman invited guests to the party, which would double as his wedding. Fifty couples gathered to help him celebrate the occasion. As the justice of the peace took his position for the ceremony, it was revealed that the "bride was a young man and that most of the wedding presents were a variety of liquors." No one seemed to mind the deception, and the party, minus wedding vows, continued for hours.

Other than a proprietorship change from J.C. Shaw to J. Ayers in October 1859, the hotel continued as a constant asset of the community, where politicians such as Galvestonian Guy Bryan—a member of the House of Representatives and former classmate of Rutherford B. Hayes—would invite the public to hear speeches and engage in debates.

In the early days of Texas's participation in the Civil War, the Galveston Zouaves were given a regiment flag, handmade by the ladies of the city, at a formal presentation held at Tremont House on July 3, 1861. The Zouaves,

Captain Baullard's company, which would eventually join Ebenezar B. Nichol's Ninth Infantry as Company C, were unique in both their training and appearance.

Based on those of skilled French soldiers from North Africa, their uniforms consisted of baggy red trousers, short braided jackets and a form of tasseled fez. The Zouaves were among the finest trained soldiers on both the Union and Confederate sides of the conflict.

At four o'clock in the afternoon, a Miss Davis represented the ladies by presenting the flag to Mr. Borrell from the company and delivering an address to attendees in French. Borrell made a reply in French to acknowledge the gift and promised to defend it. Afterward, the company and a large gathering proceeded to the cathedral, where, according to French custom, the flag was consecrated to signify the triple ties of gallantry, patriotism and religion.

The war years brought difficult times to the island, and many moved their businesses and families to Houston. At one point, a bombshell exploded in a corner of the Tremont, causing damage but no casualties.

Two of the most important events in the hotel's history—a speech given by General Sam Houston in hope of discouraging secession and a tragic fire in 1865—are detailed in later chapters of this book.

The Tremont hosted years of music, laughter, discussions of peace and war. It witnessed the days of the Republic of Texas as a sovereign state, as a state in the Union, then the Confederacy and back again.

Its history ended in flames.

# 2

# SAM HOUSTON'S PLEA

Any true Texan is familiar with the name of Sam Houston. The American general and statesman played a vital role in the Texas Revolution and became an iconic figure in the state's history. Houston served as the first and third president of the Republic of Texas and was one of the first two men to represent Texas in the U.S. Senate. He also holds the unusual honor of being the only individual to be elected governor of two different states, serving as the sixth governor of Tennessee and the seventh of Texas.

Texas became a state in 1845, and Sam Houston won his position as its governor in 1859.

With the Civil War looming, Houston disagreed with many in power that the state should align with the Confederacy, even though it was decidedly a pro-Southern state. Though he acquiesced with secession from the United States in 1861, Houston argued that the state should become a republic again rather than a member of the Confederacy.

When Sam Houston refused to take an oath of loyalty to the Confederacy, the state's Secession Convention declared the office of governor vacant, and he was evicted from office on March 16. He was offered federal assistance to prevent the removal, but he refused their aid.

Just one week after the attempt on Fort Sumter, Houston decided to make one last attempt to sway public opinion about participation in the war and took a steamboat to Galveston with the intention of making a public speech. He had already been labeled as a traitor by some newspapers in the state, and tensions were high.

City leaders worried that his arrival might start a public riot, and a committee of four of his friends met him at the wharf on April 19 to urge him not to appear.

The suggestion incensed the imposing Houston, who responded, "If I should go back home, as you suggest, it would go all over Texas that Sam Houston was scared of making a speech. No, I can't do it."

His friends accompanied him down The Strand as he nodded and smiled at onlookers, paying no attention to the unflattering remarks being shouted by some members of the crowd. Local militia and armed civilians, who called themselves the Committee on Public Safety, were a clearly visible presence along the route.

There are conflicting reports about the planned location of his speech, with

Portrait of Sam Houston (1793–1863). *Library of Congress Prints and Photographs Division, Washington D.C.*

some accounts stating that it was the courthouse and others reporting it was to have been at Dr. Hurlbut's new building in the 2200 block of Postoffice. What is certain is that neither location was prepared for a crowd the size that had gathered, so the party headed toward the Tremont House, where Houston had stayed on previous visits with his family.

At the time, there were two armories located within one block of the Tremont.

Pushing his way past the hostile crowd accompanied by his friends, he walked through the lobby and up the stairs to the second floor, where he could access the balcony looking over the street. One account reported that a threatening onlooker rushed the stairs to attack Houston but was kicked back down by another bystander.

Though the crowd was obviously not receptive to Houston's presence, his bravado and calm won them over enough to allow him to speak his mind, listening—for the most part—respectfully.

Standing on the north gallery and speaking loudly to the hundreds of people who filled the streets below, Houston shared his thoughts from the viewpoint of a man who had experienced more than his share of battle.

He eloquently warned against the horrors of war, predicting that "fire and rivers of blood" would result from the South's secession from the Union.

"Some of you laugh to scorn the idea of bloodshed as the result of secession, but let me tell you what is coming," Houston said. "Your fathers and husbands, your sons and brothers, will be herded at the point of the bayonet. While I believe with you in the doctrine of state rights…the North is determined to preserve this Union."

"After the sacrifice of countless of millions of treasure and hundreds of thousands of lives, you may win Southern independence if God not be against you, but I doubt it."

It was General Sam Houston's last public address.

If the strong words made those listening solemnly consider that fate, it wasn't enough to the change their minds.

After he finished and returned to street level, Houston inquired about the location of an officer who had shouted particularly offensive comments, but the man had retreated, possibly wanting to avoid encountering the six-foot, six-inch general face to face.

Violence had been avoided, and Houston's companions escorted him back to the wharf to board a waiting steamer to take him back to the mainland.

Sam Houston retired to Huntsville, where he passed away two years later.

One year after his speech to Galvestonians, another politician made a different type of plea from the east gallery of the Tremont. Governor Francis R. Lubbock encouraged Galvestonians to destroy their entire city except for fortifications, so that if the "vandal hordes" arrived from the north they would not be able to find shelter or potable water. The speech was not well received, and Lubbock left soon after.

# 3
# FIRE OF 1865

T he spring of 1865 brought an end to the Civil War, and on June 18, General Gordon Granger arrived at Galveston with two thousand Federal troops to occupy Texas.

The Tremont had housed Confederate troops from 1861 through 1864. In 1865, the hotel became the quarters of the Forty-Eighth and Eighty-Third Ohio and Thirty-Seventh Illinois Regiments of the Union forces.

On the afternoon of July 21, soldiers occupying the Tremont House started a fire in the third-floor garret, reportedly to cook food, and caused the mostly wooden structure to erupt in flames at 12:45 p.m.

Thick white smoke pushed through the wooden shingles, and by the time a fire company arrived, the building was engulfed in flames. Scarcity of water in the city hindered the battle, and after the wooden portion of the structure was lost, the three-story brick section and its wooden supports caught and burned as well. Bystanders later remarked on the resounding crashes of the walls falling one by one.

Within the hour, there was nothing left of the 1839 Tremont, and attention was turned to surrounding buildings, many of which were also constructed of wood.

Ramshackle buildings on the corner northeast from the hotel were quickly pulled down by the growing crowd of citizens in an attempt to stem the fire's progress.

Denis Neil's clothing store on the corner of Tremont and Market Streets and Dr. Bennett's adjoining house were in imminent danger having no barrier besides an open street from the flying embers that were blown by a wind from the south in their direction. Locals were well aware that if the shop caught fire, the entire block of wooden structures would be lost.

Heroic firemen and civilians positioned themselves on roofs and galleries and directed available streams of water from fire hoses, brought buckets of water and spread wet blankets on hot spots.

One fireman who took control of an engine hose later shared with a friend that the heat was so extreme that his tongue began to involuntarily protrude from his mouth and he lost the ability to speak.

Thomas Barnard, an ex-policeman known locally as "One-armed Tom," took the distressed fireman's place on the roof, braving the encroaching fire line.

Roofs as far away as The Strand caught fire, but thanks to the exertions of firemen, soldiers and volunteers, the damage was limited mainly to burned shingles.

The hotel ruins were a pitiful sight, with only a partial chimney left standing. It seemed a cruel addition to the suffering of a city still trying to find its way after difficult war years.

It was later discovered that liquor stores, which had been shuttered since the Union occupation, were broken into during the excitement, but telltale signs of consumption soon gave the culprits away.

There was much conjecture about whether the fire happened by design or by accident, but with no eyewitnesses, it is destined to remain one of the island's many unsolved mysteries.

A second wave of destructive fires in Galveston the first week in August were proclaimed in Southern newspapers to have been caused by "villainous design" by occupying troops, but as with the previous fire, those comments were supposition.

General Horatio Wright relieved General Granger in Galveston immediately afterward.

A newspaper editorial weeks later reminded neighbors that when wooden structures had been lost in the past, brick buildings almost immediately took their place. But it also forecast that this instance would be different, as money and materials were in short supply due to the recent war.

The prediction proved to be wrong. Tremont Street was the only road that had been shelled almost all the way to the beach, which made it an enticing thoroughfare for walks and pleasure rides and shopping trips in carriages.

# Part II

---◆---

## PRIDE OF GALVESTON

# A NEW PLAN

I n 1871, the Galveston Hotel Company, made up of a group of prominent Galveston investors, decided to erect a second Tremont House that would rival the grandeur of any hotel in the South.

With financial capital of $200,000, they commissioned architect Fred S. Steward to design the magnificent structure. Steward was well regarded as the architect of the impressive Masonic temple on Twenty-Second Street.

The plans he devised were for a four-story hotel with an impressive center rotunda, a grand double staircase and an expansive lobby that extended across half of the ground floor.

The committee purchased half of the block bounded by Tremont, Church and Twenty-Fourth Streets, along with an alley in February 1872 for $35,000, and proceeded to lay a brick foundation for the new hotel.

The long side of the structure, on Church Street, stretched a remarkable 204 feet, while the sides on Twenty-Third (Tremont) and Twenty-Fourth Streets were 120 feet. The ground floor store spaces that faced Twenty-Third and Church Streets and the rooms along Twenty-Fourth were 60 feet deep, and a generous 84-by-50-foot landscaped courtyard adjoined the alleyway.

The investors overspent their funds, and after only the first two floors of the hotel were built, construction halted.

The forsaken structure stood abandoned for two years until new owners acquired the project. The railroad building firm of Burnett & Kilpatrick, which also leased the state penitentiary building, stepped in and hired Nicholas Clayton and his partner Michael Lynch to complete the hotel.

Verkin Studio photo of Tremont Hotel, circa 1925. *Galveston Texas History Center of the Rosenberg Library, Galveston, Texas.*

Steward was brought in as a consultant, and his original plans, with the addition of a fifth floor and a mansard tower, were used.

The massive new Tremont House, billed as the only first-class hotel in the city, opened its doors in 1877, and Galveston had its new crown jewel. Clayton and Lynch returned to carry out rehabilitation projects to the hotel in 1884 and 1896.

# ENVY OF THE SOUTH

The grand opening of the new Tremont House in 1877 was celebrated by the entire state. The tallest structure in the city, it was the first thing to be spotted by visitors arriving by land or sea and was designed to make an impression. Hundreds of craftsmen had worked to bring the architects' design to reality and did justice to every breathtaking detail.

The four-story hotel was constructed of an estimated two million bricks covered in stucco to replicate pristine white stonework.

Its lowest story showcased a cast-iron front supported by Corinthian columns that flanked tall, slender windows topped with arches ornamented with oak leaf design keystones.

Two iron Corinthian columns of larger proportions than the rest supported an entablature over the main entrance, underneath which was a French plate transom glass with the words "Tremont Hotel" in gold lettering.

Upper stories featured quoin-cornered rusticated masonry, centered with projections flanking the entrances on each side that continued to the roofline.

The hoods and corbels in the upper windows were finished with an oak leaf cluster under the end of each arch. The Tremont boasted 325 windows set with the finest French plate glass.

The Tremont's famous mansard roof was adorned with colored Scotch slate, placed in a pattern of diamonds, and each side of the center was pierced with six dormered windows. Cresting around the roof was painted an elegant ultramarine blue lipped with gold that shone in the island sunlight.

High above the front center of the roof perched the Tremont's trademark observatory, where the finest views of the island could be enjoyed. The bravest of visitors could access the observatory railing, 96 feet above street level, by venturing through a trap door and climbing up a small wooden ladder. Across the top of the front window of the room, facing the street, was a spread-eagle emblem whose wingspan stretched five and a half feet. The flagpole atop the structure sported a flag that announced, "Tremont Hotel."

Far below at street level, a gracious 242-foot wooden awning wrapped around the hotel to shelter visitors from the elements. According to insurance documents and Sanborn maps, the property also had a two-story servants' building on the southwest corner of the lot, with an 18-by-84-foot footprint.

A separate brick building housed a Bacon's Improved Trunk Engine that provided steam heat and power for the elevator and other mechanizations, and a two-story brick smokestack on a brick base stood to its rear.

# First Floor

As guests passed through the Tremont Street entrance of the hotel, they entered a twenty-four-foot-wide, forty-eight-foot-long vestibule flanked by four store spaces, two on each side. The larger of the spaces on the north side, at thirty-two feet wide, was a shop for gentlemen's furnishings.

Once through the hallway, they encountered a breathtaking fifty-four-by-seventy-two-foot lobby, haloed with an octagonal rotunda. The floors of the hallway and rotunda were covered with white-veined Italian and black American marble tiles.

Lighting was initially provided by gas fixtures that were only necessary at night. During the day, light streamed down through the rotunda from a spectacular skylight, emanating into the corridors and meeting the light entering through windows.

Southern hotels took the issue of ventilation seriously, and the Tremont allowed breezes from the Gulf to circulate through windows, down wide hallways and by means of Hay's patent skylight ventilator that could be opened or closed as desired.

Graceful Corinthian columns supported an upper gallery that overlooked the frescoed lobby, which was surrounded by smaller rooms, including the one for the hotel vaults, a brush room, baggage storage and a steam-powered guest elevator.

First floor interior of Tremont House. *Galveston Texas History Center of the Rosenberg Library, Galveston, Texas.*

A reception desk to the right was sheltered beneath the grand staircase that was adorned with a bronze statue of Diana, the Roman goddess of the hunt, on its newel post.

Locals and visitors could congregate in a large area with seating provided as a place to see others and be seen.

A separate ladies' Church Street entrance was located just past the lobby area and protected female guests from being "overwhelmed" by the business of male-dominated areas with their spittoons, brass footrails, cigar smoke and saloons. To the right of this small stairwell and hallway was a shop, and to the left was an inviting forty-three-by-twenty-four-foot reading room where visitors could browse the local newspapers or catch up on correspondence.

Just beyond the reading room was the Tremont Barber Shop off a hallway with windows facing the courtyard and men's restrooms outfitted with fine Italian marble washbasins.

After gentlemen visitors spruced up in the barbershop, they could meander to the adjoining saloon and billiards parlor, which could also be

Bartenders at the Tremont House Bar. *Galveston Texas History Center of the Rosenberg Library, Galveston, Texas.*

accessed through the Twenty-Fourth Street entrance. It was an impressive seventy-four-by-twenty-four-foot men's retreat featuring a frescoed ceiling supported by Corinthian columns and furnished with heavily upholstered chairs and eleven billiard tables.

Of decidedly less interest to guests, the hotel office, steam-powered laundry and baggage storage occupied the space on the other side of the rear entrance.

Visitors who ventured into the courtyard were treated to a handsomely landscaped area divided into four sections, surrounding a twenty-two-foot fountain. Topping a fifteen-foot-diameter basin of water was a pedestal of dolphin statues that spouted water from their mouths. Above them, three mermaids with aquatic plants at their feet held a large shell in the air.

With the first floor designed mostly for business purposes, the second floor was conceived to become the center of the hotel's social life with parlors, dining rooms, reception rooms, en suite rooms and bridal chambers.

Tremont House billiards parlor. *Galveston Texas History Center of the Rosenberg Library, Galveston, Texas.*

## SECOND FLOOR

Coming from the lobby area, guests could ascend to the second floor by way of the grand marble stairway or an elaborate steam elevator, almost eight by nine feet in size. It was one of the most newsworthy additions once the third and fourth floors were added. Stepping inside the elevator, which was basically a small furnished parlor, guests could sit on the sofa or chairs as an operator maneuvered the wondrous vehicle to the desired floor. The mechanism was even equipped with large springs meant to cushion an unexpectedly rapid descent if the supporting cables malfunctioned.

Once on the second story, a view across the elegant railings surrounding the rotunda and down onto the lobby was irresistible. Those who then glanced upward would see the immense glass dome crowning the hotel.

To the guests' right as they exited the elevator and entered the grand hall was a series of rooms that had access to a balcony facing Church Street. The largest was the main dining room, more than forty-three by eighty feet in size with an impressive twenty-foot-high ceiling and frescoed walls. In addition to thirty windows, the room had ventilators in the ceiling to ensure the comfort of guests.

Next came a modest twenty-two-foot-square private dining room and two others twelve feet, six inches by eighteen feet in size that were to be used for smaller groups. The three rooms were designed with the ability to open onto one another to adjust to any size gathering that desired to use them.

The designers of the hotel took into consideration the number of meals that would need to be prepared to serve the guests in the multiple dining rooms and provided the staff with a fifty-seven-by-thirty-five-foot kitchen at the rear of the large dining room, appointed with the best equipment of the day. In addition to a twenty-seven-foot-long Imperial cooking range, the space boasted five fireplaces (three covered and two open), four large and two small ovens, two warming areas, two thirty-four-inch-wide broilers and a dumbwaiter capable of lifting three hundred pounds.

The second floor also offered a gentleman's parlor: a large room where undoubtedly many cigars were enjoyed and business deals bartered.

Tremont House dining room and waiters. *Galveston Texas History Center of the Rosenberg Library, Galveston, Texas.*

Beside it was the elegant ladies' parlor, a slightly larger room on the corner of Tremont and Church that afforded the "fair sex" to visit with each other without the interruption of men. It was ornamented with frescoes, mirrors and decorative furnishings.

Bedecked in an Arabian Night splendor motif, the Bridal Chamber at the Tremont became a prized location, considering there were almost always several honeymooning couples staying at the hotel at the same time. The lucky couples who spent the night in the spacious, exotic suite would definitely have something to write home about.

Additional rooms on the floor were designed as spaces that would become the regular gathering places of many organizations, including one that became the regular meeting room of the Galveston Chamber of Commerce.

The second floor also housed fourteen guest chambers and three large apartments.

## Third and Fourth Floors

The third and fourth floors were each divided into forty-two large apartments and varied in size from twelve by twenty-three feet to twenty-five by twenty-one feet. This was about 50 percent larger than most southern hotels and double the size of many northern establishments of the era and thought to be quite a treat.

All but two rooms on each floor had windows, which was preferable in the days before air-conditioning to take advantage of Gulf breezes. Wide twelve-foot hallways and fourteen-foot-high ceilings also aided in circulation.

Courtyard views were afforded to eleven rooms and courtyard-facing windows to another twenty-nine.

Separate ladies' and gentlemen's water closets, or bathrooms, were located on each floor. An additional ten apartments, half on the third floor and half on the fourth, had the luxury of private bathrooms.

Linen storage closets for the entire hotel were discreetly situated on the second floor, ensuring that chambermaids had plenty of exercise on the stairs.

# TOP FLOOR

Behind the slopes of the Tremont's distinctive mansard roof lay thirty-five small servants' sleeping quarters, seven apartments and one bathroom each for ladies and gentlemen. It was also the location of twenty-five cast-iron water tanks, each of which held two thousand gallons, that were connected to pipes to provide water to apartment wash stands, the barbershop, bathrooms and kitchen. Any surplus water was directed to a large cistern for storage.

Five other rooms on the top floor were dedicated to long-term storage of trunks.

Floors on every level of the hotel were deadened with Virginia cane fiber felt beneath the carpeting to reduce the noise of the wooden floors.

Each guest room door was equipped with a safety hotel lock, following the example of the Grand Central Hotel in New York City, which was said to be impossible to pick from the outside when locked from within.

Altogether, the five floors of Tremont House equaled about two and one-sixth acres of space, each inch of which had been precisely planned and utilized.

# 6

# GRAND INITIAL BALL

When the second Tremont House opened its doors, arrangements were finally made to welcome its architects back to the city to celebrate their accomplishment with a Grand Initial Ball and Supper in May 1877. Hotel manager J. Harvey Pierce sent a letter to J.H. Burnett and Robert Kilpatrick, the principals of the firm who completed the construction, and requested that they choose an appropriate date for the event. The letter was signed by a lengthy list of prominent businessmen. A Thursday evening, May 3, was chosen, just two weeks after the letter was sent, and arrangements were quickly made.

The description of the occasion appeared in the local newspaper the next day, making any reader who did not attend envious.

As they entered the brightly lit interior, finely dressed attendees were greeted with the sight of flags draped from each second-floor railing surrounding the rotunda and one large flag suspended on a rope drawn across the circular opening.

On the second floor, the main dining rooms and adjacent private dining rooms were opened to create one magnificent space decorated with evergreens and flags. The tables were ornamented with flower pyramids and trays of edible delicacies.

After the meal, the dining room was converted into a ballroom for the remainder of the evening.

Richard Maddern's Lone Star Band, considered one of the finest brass bands in the South, provided music from the bandstand at the end of the

Carriages outside of the Tremont House. *Galveston County Museum, Galveston Texas.*

dining hall. Maddern, a talented musician himself, had previously conducted the orchestra at Galveston's Opera House and the Varieties Theatre in New Orleans. The program of the evening included sixteen dances and four promenades, with a welcome refreshment break arriving just before the eleventh dance at midnight.

Among distinguished gentlemen noted on the dance floor were General Mariano Escobedo, a Mexican military leader; Congressman John Henninger Reagan of Texas; and Mayor James Henry French of San Antonio. A large group of invited San Antonio socialites attended as well.

Successful Galveston businessmen, lawyers, bankers and merchants also made an appearance. Easily recognizable faces at the time included Julius Runge, Marx Marx, Harris Kempner, Felix Halff, Henry Seeligson, Theodore Ayers, Moritz Kopperl, James Moreau Brown, George Sealy, Leon Blum, Joseph Graham Goldthwaite, Marcus Mott, Noah Noble John, J.D. Skinner and others.

Many of the guests stayed at the Tremont overnight, paying the regular rate of three dollars per room.

It was the first of many grand balls and society events that would be hosted by the stunning hotel.

# 7
# ARCHITECT
# NICHOLAS J. CLAYTON

A native of County Cork, Ireland, Nicholas Joseph Clayton was born in 1839. When he was nine years old, he and his mother immigrated to Cincinnati, Ohio, following his father's death.

He began his career as a plasterer and worked in Cincinnati, New Orleans, Louisville, Memphis and St. Louis before serving three years in the U.S. Navy during the Civil War.

After he returned to Cincinnati following the war, he worked as a marble carver and architectural draftsman.

In 1872, Clayton relocated to Galveston after being hired by Memphis, Tennessee architectural firm Jones and Baldwin to become the supervising architect for the First Presbyterian Church and the second Tremont Hotel.

He remained in Galveston, and his High Victorian designs had such an effect on the island's architecture during the following three decades that locals refer to as the Golden Era, that it is sometimes referred to as the Clayton Era. His distinctive, bold style, attention to detail and decorative brick and ironwork are easily recognizable.

He received numerous commissions to design churches and other religious institutions across Texas and in Louisiana, the first of which was St. Mary's Church (now St. Mary's Cathedral) in Austin in 1873.

Among those still in existence in Galveston are St. Patrick's Church (1874–77) and reconstruction (1901–2), Eaton Memorial Chapel (1878–79), Grace Episcopal Church (1894–95) and the dome of the second Sacred Heart Church (1910).

One of Clayton's early important public buildings was the 1881 Galveston Electric Pavilion on the beachfront between Twenty-First and Twenty-Third Streets. It was the first building in Texas with electric lighting and became one of the earliest tourist beach attractions, offering "fresh beer, excellent music and fine lunches." It was later lost in a fire.

In 1887 Clayton served on an advisory board during the construction of the problematic dome on the state capitol building in Austin and was responsible for determining the capitol's furnishings the following year.

At the age of fifty-two, Clayton married thirty-year-old Galvestonian Mary Lorena Ducie on July 6, 1891. They had five children.

A great number of the architect's residential and commercial creations have been defaced or altered over the years, and even more have been lost to destruction or demolition. Thankfully, others have survived for future generations to enjoy.

A few of his Galveston creations that can still be appreciated in person are H.M. Trueheart and Company Building (1881–82), Gresham House (also known as Bishop's Palace, 1885–92), Clarke and Courts Building (1890), Ashbel Smith Building at University of Texas Medical Branch (also known as "Old Red," 1891), Hutchings-Sealy Building (1895–96), James Fadden Building (1896–97) and Star Drug Store Building (1886, 1909).

The respected designer was a founding member of the Texas State Association of Architects and a fellow of the American Institute of Architects, but his business suffered after 1900.

A lengthy lawsuit involving controversy concerning the awarding of the contract for a new Galveston County Courthouse, and a drop in prosperity following the 1900 Storm essentially ended his dynamic career.

Clayton declared bankruptcy in March 1903 and, although he continued to work, was never awarded another significant commission.

As he attempted to repair a crack in his home's chimney in November 1916, the candle he held caught his undershirt on fire and he was severely burned. While

Portrait of architect Nicholas Joseph Clayton (1840–1916). *Galveston Texas History Center of the Rosenberg Library, Galveston, Texas.*

recovering from the injuries, Clayton developed pneumonia and passed away the first week of December.

It would seem that a man who created such grand structures would have an equally grand monument at his grave in Calvary Catholic Cemetery, but that is not the case. His widow was distressed about the fact that one could not be afforded, to which their close friend Rabbi Henry Cohen replied that it wasn't necessary. "He has them all over town. Just go and read some of the cornerstones."

# 8

# TREMONT YEARS 1877–1928

T remont House was considered officially open following the grand ball honoring Burnett & Kilpatrick, the contractors who succeeded in finishing its construction, but that wasn't the first celebration held there.

The evening before its official first ball, the hotel was the site of an impromptu dance. Two days later, an evening ball was held for a large party from San Antonio, including that city's mayor. It was not unusual for the hotel to have two or three public events every week, in addition to private parties and receptions.

In spite of a sometimes-confusing procession of ever-changing owners, proprietors, managers, and staff, Tremont House would be the undeniable social center of the city for more than half a century.

In the tradition of the first Tremont House, countless celebrities and distinguished guests would visit the hotel. Six presidents are known to have visited the hotel: Rutherford B. Hayes, Ulysses S. Grant, Grover Cleveland, Benjamin Harrison, James A. Garfield and Chester A. Arthur. Other guests included celebrities and dignitaries like President A. Diaz of Mexico, Secretary of the Interior H.J. Lamar, Vice President William A. Wheeler, state senators, state legislators, military leaders, ballerina Anna Pavlova, Prince Jerome Napoleon Bonaparte, Governor James Stephen Hogg, William H. Vanderbilt, European nobility and an assortment of luminaries over five decades.

Stereoview of Tremont House on Tremont Street. *Galveston Texas History Center of the Rosenberg Library, Galveston, Texas.*

# 1877

Though some sources claim that the first few sessions of Agricultural and Mechanical College of Texas were held at the Tremont before there was a campus in Bryan, there is no conclusive evidence to prove it. There is, however, a Texas A&M University connection that Aggies, students and alumni of the university will enjoy.

Bernard Sbisa (pronounced speez-uh) was an Austrian immigrant chef who took over management of the Tremont House in May 1877 through the partnership of Sbiza & Orfila after their previous establishment, the

Grand Southern Hotel, was lost in a fire earlier that year. They immediately enacted changes in the way the hotel was operated and the prices charged. In particular, they noted that "servants and employees that have enjoyed an excess of freedom have to be brought under rule."

Employees may have been relieved then, when just a few months later in December, the partners gave up their lease at the Tremont to move to other opportunities.

Sbisa moved to Bryan to manage Steward's Hall at the agricultural college in its third year of operation. He became the school's steward of subsistence and was in charge of feeding the four hundred cadets housed in the two buildings on campus, Old Main and the mess hall. The mess was originally named Steward's, then renamed Gathright Hall in honor of A&M's first president. After that building was lost to fire, a new mess named Sbisa Hall was constructed in 1913, after the chef who spent the rest of his life feeding the students.

In June 1877, when court proceedings and investigations were being held regarding a Galveston fire, ladies who were summoned as witnesses were called to the Tremont House sitting room to be interviewed "to provide them with more convenience and comfort" than going to the courthouse.

The first few months Tremont House was open, the engineering team used coal to produce the gas required to light the building, but that changed on July 9, 1877. That day, W.J. Rice placed a new Maxim Gas Machine in place that promised to power one hundred lights. Burnett and Kilpatrick had ordered it after learning of its success in lighting numerous northern hotels, factories and churches over the previous six years.

Instead of using coal for gas production, the machine made by Welch & Lawson of New York used gasoline. At twenty-five cents per gallon, this change would provide significant savings to the hotel.

A version of the Maxim had been installed the week prior at the *News* offices, and night shift printers agreed to its success.

Samuel Lawson of Welch & Lawson, builder of the machines, was present to oversee the substitution of the new for the old machinery. Unfortunately, plumbing connections installed in the days prior were improperly done and caused several delays. The gas was finally turned on at 6:30 p.m., and the public was invited to return at dark to witness the entire hotel lighted by the new method.

Amateur horticulturalists flocked to the parlors of Tremont house on the evening of October 3, 1877, for a special treat. Noah Noble John, an employee of William Hendley and Company, exhibited a rare night-blooming cereus with two fragrant, pale white flowers. Known as "Queen of the Night," this variety of cactus blooms only once per year. The gathering was so enthusiastically attended that John, who had an extensive collection of rare tropical plants, promised to return within two weeks with another variety to share.

That same week, bricklayer George Birrs completed work on the largest cistern in Texas for the Tremont, with a reservoir capacity of 186,000 gallons of water. Once soil was replaced atop the construction in the courtyard, the hotel planted a beautiful flower garden that became a destination for romantic strolls on the island.

Two weeks later, the Tremont appeared in the headlines again when the saloon's bartender, William Boddeker, caught a thief. He had noticed shortages of small change in his cash drawer for some time and suspected the bottle washer of helping himself to the coins. Boddeker set a clever trap that involved the use of a tack, string and bottle, rigged so the bottle would fall if the till drawer was opened. Once ready, he casually strolled into the billiards saloon to await the results. The bottle soon fell and shattered some glassware, which alerted the bartender, who ran back to find the drawer open and the culprit cowering behind the bar. He was immediately reprimanded and fired.

Another theft from the hotel by an employee ended up in court several months earlier, when Charles Wirtz was accused of taking a spoon from the hotel.

# 1878

The new year began with John F. Elliott & Co. acting as proprietors of the hotel. A Mr. O'Hanlon ran the front office, Richard Sommers was in charge of cuisine and James Moore managed the billiards parlor. New owners in the coming months resulted in changes in personnel, after which only Moore remained.

Marx Marx and Harris Kempner purchased the Tremont House from the Tremont Hotel Company on May 28, 1878. They renovated the hotel, installed new carpeting and furnishings throughout the hotel and hired George McGinley to manage it. McGinley had previously managed the Grand National Hotel in Jacksonville, Florida, and the Kimball House in Atlanta, Georgia. He hired a well-known chef named Beauclerc and his

Miles & Pinkard postcard of men standing at Tremont House lobby desk, circa 1905. *Author's collection.*

Brass key fobs from Tremont House, circa 1920s. *Photo by author. Item courtesy of Rosenberg Library Museum, Galveston, Texas.*

corps of assistants to run the kitchen, which made the Tremont a favored destination for French cuisine.

Tremont House offered an in-house ticket office with agent Starr S. Jones for the convenience of guests who needed to travel by ship or rail.

# 1879

Before Ellis Island opened in 1892, hundreds of thousands of immigrants arrived in America, passing through the Port of Galveston. It's one of the reasons that the city has had such a multicultural and colorful past.

French entrepreneur Baron George de Pardonnet checked into the Tremont House on May 22, 1879. He had already achieved notoriety overseas thanks to publishing pamphlets and a book that provided immigrants from his homeland with all the necessary information concerning how to move to America and settle in Kansas. This visit to Galveston was related to meetings to set up partnerships with Texas railways for the same purpose. He made his fortune guiding those seeking their own.

Texas's Governor Oran Milo Roberts and his wife, Frances, stayed at the Tremont Hotel on July 25 of that year to attend a conference with the Board of Health.

In response to yellow fever outbreaks in Mexico and the states of the United States that bordered it, the Texas legislature created the Texas Quarantine Department on April 10, 1879 (later renamed the Texas Department of Public Health and Vital Statistics in 1903).

Roberts attended an informal reception in the parlors of the hotel upon his arrival. A champagne toast was given by Mayor Leonard, which initiated a stream of other toasts until the dinner hour. It was an especially social affair considering that a quarantine had recently been lifted, but Galveston was held up as an example to other Texans as a city whose successful quarantines and other measures stemmed the spread of the disease.

A popular urban legend at the time was that a dog had jumped from the tower of the Tremont House and survived. As improbable a scenario as it was, the fact that no one could ever locate the dog who achieved the act did not discourage others from trying to repeat the feat. Fortunately, the local dog pound charged two dollars per animal at the time, which was more than any of the bragging rights competitors were willing to spend.

# 1880–1890

Insurance man William Francis Beers later remembered that he and his wife, Iola, were exceedingly impressed by the Tremont and its guest rooms when they honeymooned there in 1880, stating he "thought it was heaven."

They boarded at the hotel for two years, after which the couple built their own large home, which they modeled after the Tremont.

Several well-known authors also visited the Tremont, and most were well-received. That was not the case during a visit by Oscar Wilde in June 1882.

Wilde, who had already published a book of poetry but had yet to pen his most famous works, arrived during an eight-month-long lecture tour throughout the United States. His topic in Galveston concerned the Decorative Arts, which was not a popular subject but managed to sell out, in spite of the high ticket price, due to enthusiastic press announcements. The event was held at Nicholas Clayton's Electric Pavilion.

His lengthy presentation was pronounced to be a failure. The author spoke in a monotone voice, seeming to be disinterested in the topic himself, and many attendees left before the lecture concluded. The poor acoustics of

Galveston Cycling Club posing in front of the Tremont House. *Galveston Texas History Center of the Rosenberg Library, Galveston, Texas.*

the pavilion, which wasn't designed for the purpose of lectures, probably did not help matters.

At noon on September 7, 1885, a meeting was called in the reading room of the Tremont to discuss the establishment of a home for maimed and disabled Confederate veterans and their families, to be built in Austin. Colonel William L. Moody and H.W. Rhodes proposed the formation of a Galveston branch association of the veterans of the John H. Hood Camp in Austin, which was unanimously accepted. Annual dues of $1.50 were set, so that members of all means could afford to participate.

With the goal of providing assistance in raising funds for the home, they also invited Mrs. Val C. Giles, a female representative of the camp from Austin who was then at the Tremont, to extend an invitation to the women of Galveston to participate as well. The well-attended ladies' meeting was held in the reading room at 6:00 p.m. that same evening.

The Texas Confederate Home opened in November 1886.

In response to the popularity of the new trend of roller skating, The Tremont temporarily converted its billiards hall at the rear of the hotel into a private rink and opened it as a place for members only in 1887.

Tremont House was the full-time residence of several doctors, including Dr. S.M. Welch and Dr. Ashey W. Fly, who would later become mayor of Galveston and lead the charge to clean up city corruption. Both men had offices on Postoffice Street.

# 1890–1900

An ambitious young businessman named Clarence Henry Gueringer became the new proprietor of the Tremont in March 1896, after signing a five-year lease. He at once set to the task of reinvigorating the hotel's appearance and reputation, which had flagged in recent years.

The two hundred south and east rooms were repainted, the bar was stocked with fine liquors and a well-known mixologist was hired, and fire escapes were installed on all sides of the building.

Gueringer also ordered eight of the latest Brunswick Balke–patterned tables for the billiards room, which had been closed for several years. When the hall was reopened, it quickly filled with cheerful, grateful guests.

The following month, when Galveston's Beach Hotel went on the block of a sheriff's sale, Gueringer bid to purchase it, but lost to Dallas's Colonel

W.E. Hughes, owner of the Tremont and Windsor Hotel Company—the same company that had purchased the Tremont House.

That year, in addition to managing the Tremont, Gueringer became proprietor of the Beach Hotel and Houston's Hutchins House, where he had begun his career as a night clerk.

He traveled extensively in North America to promote tourism to Galveston, and even took pamphlets to distribute during his Denver honeymoon after his Halloween 1896 wedding to twenty-four-year-old divorcée Mary Martinez Selby.

The dining room of Tremont House that December was reported to be one of the most desired places to enjoy Christmas dinner. Chef Cleofas F. Smith served guests mouthwatering selections of pompano (fish) filets, roast beef, venison, turkey, sweetbreads, chicken, quail, terrapin, antelope, prairie chicken, wild goose, canvasback duck, pâté de foie gras, ice creams, puddings, confections and vegetables. Barkeeper A. Senz provided the finest wines and locally brewed Pabst beer. It was, in every respect, a bountiful feast.

Dinner plate from Tremont House dining room. *Photo by author. Item courtesy of Rosenberg Library Museum, Galveston, Texas.*

James Lewis Malone, one of the top five international billiards players of the 1880s and 1890s, arrived at Tremont House late on a Saturday night, February 6, 1897. Malone was so nationally recognized and respected for his talent that his likeness was featured on cigarette trading cards in 1887 and 1888, in a series titled "World Champions."

He met with hotel manager Gueringer the following Wednesday to arrange an exhibition game in the rotunda of the Tremont. James J. Moore, manager of the hotel billiards hall for over twenty years, made all of the arrangements. The event was well attended, and due to the fact that the rotunda ran from the ground floor to the skylight, a billiards table was moved to the center of the area so it could be viewed from the railings overlooking the games from every floor.

The hotel quartered soldiers during the Spanish-American War in 1898 and again in 1917 and 1918 during the First World War.

# 1900–1928

Governor Joseph Draper Sayers visited Galveston in April 1900 to be present at the unveiling of the seventy-four-foot-high Texas Heroes Monument that commemorates those who fought in the Texas Revolution.

He arrived to find his rooms at the Tremont House beautifully decorated with flower arrangements courtesy of the Daughters of the Republic of Texas, who had invited him as a guest for the event.

His first visit to the hotel had been twenty years earlier, when, as lieutenant governor, he made a public address in front of the hotel on July 21, 1880, campaigning to save public lands for homesteaders and schools.

On September 8, 1900, a hurricane that still stands as the nation's deadliest natural disaster struck the island. It is referred to as the 1900 Storm. Though over eight thousand people perished and a large portion of Galveston was leveled, the Tremont House became a refuge and saved the lives of everyone inside. The story of what happened inside and outside of the Tremont is detailed in another chapter dedicated entirely to the tragedy.

In February 1901, George Korst, who was proprietor during the 1900 Storm, resigned his position at the hotel, sharing that he had never fully gotten over the nervous strain caused by the hurricane. He had opened the property to whoever needed shelter and in the aftermath did everything in his power to remain calm and be of assistance to the community. Korst was greatly respected and remembered fondly after his move to New York.

Dr. William Gammon, a physician and surgeon, and George Sealy Ewalt, secretary and treasurer of the Brush Electric Light Company of Galveston, partnered to purchase the Tremont House in 1902.

The proprietorship was leased to an interesting group of sisters named Fisher, who had previous experience successfully operating hotels. They remained in that position from 1902 to 1907, with William Easton as hotel manager. The contentious relationship between Gammon, Ewalt and the Fishers is detailed in a separate chapter.

With the city well on the way to recovery after the 1900 Storm, some of the favorite activities of Galvestonians made appearances again, including Christmas dinner at the Tremont in 1907.

The menu reflected the international tastes of the guests and the heritages of the kitchen staff: Blue Point oysters on the half shell, Russian caviar en Bellevue, pickled walnuts, green sea turtle à la Delmonico, salted pecans, Consomme Printaniere Royal, stuffed olives, broiled Spanish mackerel au Beurre Montpeltier, Pommes de Terre Duchess, frog legs in bread crumbs with tartar sauce, turkey with clam stuffing and cranberry jelly, asparagus au Beurre Fondere, cauliflower with sauce supreme, Fillet de Bouef Pique aux Champignons, baked mashed potatoes, French peas, suckling pig with baked apples, champagne punch, anisette wafers, pâté de foie gras à la Strasburg, lobster salad en mayonnaise, roasted canvasback duck with French prunes, stuffed tomatoes and dressed lettuce.

After dinner, guests were treated to Christmas plum pudding with hard cognac sauce, hot mince pie, orange meringue pie, Vienna Charlotte Russe, pomegranate jelly, fruitcake, angel cake and Neapolitan ice cream, along with Roquefort, Neufchatel and edam cheeses, Saratoga flakes (crackers), raisins, assorted nuts and confectioneries and café noir Française.

Once the Fisher sisters were no longer on site, Gammon moved into the Tremont in 1908 with his wife, Theresa, whom he had married the year before purchasing the property.

At that time, the hotel was a popular stopping place for salesmen, who could make use of the parlors as temporary sample rooms.

Gammon closed the original second-floor dining room that seated 360 guests and opened a café on the first floor. The doctor then proceeded to convert the entire second floor into a twenty-eight-room private apartment for his family.

Gammon and Ewalt spent approximately $100,000 in 1910 to remodel and update the hotel, less than ten years after the last of the repairs from the 1900 Storm were completed. The Galveston Hotel Company, which had been instrumental in building the Tremont, was focused on constructing a grand beach hotel at that time named the Hotel Galvez on top of the new seawall, which would create significant competition for clientele.

Hot and cold running water was added to each room, and the washstands and pitchers disappeared into the community. Twenty-five bathrooms were also added, most connected "Jack and Jill style" connecting two rooms.

The Gammon's first child, a daughter named Mary Francis, was born in August 1911 but sadly passed away of pneumonia at the hotel in 1912 less than a week before Christmas.

The following December, their son William Jr. was born, joined by a daughter Marjory three years later. With an entire hotel to roam, the children played ball in the hallways and rode bicycles in the ballroom.

Meetings of stockholders of the Galveston Ruby Mining Company held evening meetings in the reading room of the Tremont House, where they elected officers and planned projects, including work on several claims

Egg cup from Tremont House dining room. *Photo by author.* *Item courtesy of Rosenberg Library Museum, Galveston, Texas.*

Postcard showing bird's-eye view overlooking city park with Tremont House on right, circa 1900. *Galveston Texas History Center of the Rosenberg Library, Galveston, Texas.*

in Colorado. The directors of the organization were prominent local businessmen such as Charles L. Cleveland, Henry Sayles, Marx Marx, John P. Davie, Charles Vidor, Emile E. Steger and H.C. Stone

Since the great hotel had opened, its dining and public rooms continued to host regular meetings of the Galveston Chamber of Commerce and organizations in town. Great plans for railroads and businesses were proposed, generations of wedding receptions and celebrations and brainstormed solutions to health issues and disasters had all taken place there.

A combination of troublesome economy and the arrival of more modern accommodations on the island such as the Jean Laffite Hotel sealed the fate of the Tremont House as the Roaring Twenties came to a close. The opulence that was once so desirable became dated and fell out of favor.

On Halloween night 1928, George Ewalt ushered the last guests of a Washington Guards reunion to the front door and locked it behind them. A grand and elegant chapter of Galveston's history had ended.

# 9

# SHOWMAN BUFFALO BILL CODY

Imagine the excitement caused by a Native American chief, plainsmen cowboys and Indian agents striding into the lobby of the elegant Tremont Hotel. It must have been quite a sight and surprisingly one that happened more than once thanks to visits by Buffalo Bill Cody and his fellow performers.

Dime novelist Ned Buntline published a serialized account in *New York Weekly* in 1869 that presented an elaborate account of Cody's larger-than-life experiences as a buffalo hunter, fur trapper, U.S. Army scout, Pony Express rider and Indian fighter. The stories were picked up by newspapers across the nation and the world, making the handsomely rugged adventurer an international celebrity.

In the years before he established his iconic Wild West show, William Frederick Cody, better known as the showman Buffalo Bill, and his troupe of performers presented lavish indoor shows depicting thrilling and fanciful live-action depictions of life in the unsettled West.

Buffalo Bill's Combination Acting Troupe first visited the island from November 22 to 25, 1875. In those days, a "combination" was a theatrical collaboration between a star and supporting actors.

Their western melodrama, titled *The Scouts of the Plains*, was performed four times at the Tremont Opera House and thrilled audiences with vignettes of danger, suspense and triumph with a large cast of cowboys, Native Americans, sharpshooters and animals.

Touring with the troupe was one of the most unique couples of the nineteenth century: Texas Jack and Peerless Morlacchi.

Portrait of William "Buffalo Bill" Cody (1846–1917). *Courtesy of the McCracken Research Library, Buffalo Bill Center of the West, Cody, Wyoming.*

John Baker "Texas Jack" Omohundro was a former Confederate army scout turned Texas cowboy who drove cattle on some of the state's most famous trails. He later worked as a U.S. government scout in Nebraska, where he met Cody, and eventually joined his combination show.

His wife was Giuseppina "Josephine" Morlacchi, a native of Milan, Italy, known by her show name the Peerless Morlacchi. The diminutive dancer was a classically trained world-class prima ballerina and choreographer who, for a time, performed with Cody's shows, appearing as Pale Dove—an Italian-accented Native American maiden habitually in need of rescue.

After meeting on tour with the show, the tall, handsome Omohundro won the heart of the young dancer, despite her proposals of marriage from numerous wealthy suitors on the East Coast. They were married in 1873 and remained married until his death seven years later.

Texas Jack was visited by many friends during the trip to Texas and proudly introduced his beautiful bride to men who were eager to prove to their children that they knew him "back in the day."

Cody, Texas Jack and Morlacchi stayed at Tremont House during their 1875 visit, causing quite a stir with their theatrical clothing.

The next time Cody returned to Galveston, in December 1879, his popular biography *The Life of Buffalo Bill* was newly released, and the audiences' anticipation of seeing the hero in person was obvious.

Excitement grew as a grand street parade led by Cody's military brass orchestra marched through town, featuring all of its stars on horseback.

During three nightly shows and a matinee, the opera house was filled with audiences anxious to see the new show *Knight of the Plains* or *Buffalo Bill's Best Trail.* Members of the Ponca and Pawnee tribes in their native costumes performed alongside cowboys and soldiers in tableaus featuring a prairie fire, stagecoach robbery, Plains buffaloes, dances, and rifle marksmanship, thrilling onlookers, who seemed especially happy whenever Buffalo Bill "got the drop" on a "bad guy."

Attendees to the show were encouraged to purchase copies of his biography from ushers at the end of performances.

To this day, handwritten proof of the cast members' visit to Tremont House remains.

The book referred to as the register of Tremont House was not one that guests would sign as they checked into the hotel, as one would assume. It was reserved for adventurous guests and visitors who were brave enough to climb through a trapdoor and up a narrow wooden ladder to the observation tower of the hotel. In addition to the reward of unparalleled views of the city and the bay, those adventurers had the opportunity to sign the observatory register as proof they had been there. Guests occasionally included remarks about the view and the experience of reaching such an impressive height.

During their 1879 visit, several members of Buffalo Bill's combination show braved the trip to the tower and left their signatures in the book, which is now in the collection of the Galveston and Texas History Center at Galveston's Rosenberg Library.

Among those who signed were Charles A. Burgess, a government interpreter for the Sioux and one of the show's young producers; J.H. Harvey, the master of transportation; Wite (sic) Eagle (White Eagle) and Spotted Horse, members of the Sioux tribe; Ernest Green; Edward Martin; Delancey Barclay, an actor who once performed with Edwin Booth; Nellie Jones Barclay; Alex McCarthy; Frank W. Stevens; and actress Lydia Denier. Some of the signers who were lucky enough to be accommodated at the hotel added "staying at the Tremont" beside their names. Many stayed in private rail cars or camped.

Other members of the troupe, including Harry Reynolds, Buffalo Bill and others who were known to have stayed at Tremont House, did not sign the register.

By the time Cody returned on October 23, 1902, he had a new outdoor production, titled *Buffalo Bill's Wild West and the Congress of Rough Riders of the World*, featuring five hundred horses. Store owner F.E. Mistrot at Twenty-Fourth and Mechanic offered one ticket to the show for each child's suit or men's suit purchased as a sales promotion.

Cody and the principals of the show quartered at the familiar Tremont House during their engagement.

A combination of Buffalo Bill's Wild West and Pawnee Bill's Far East Combination Exhibition arrived for one day of two shows on the island in November 1910.

The month before the performance, S.H. Fielder, the agent for Buffalo Bill and Pawnee Bill, petitioned the city for permission to erect covered tents on the vacant ground on Avenue E between Thirty-Third and Thirty-Fifth Streets to be used for stables and staff dining rooms. Additional waterproof canopies were erected over the seating areas surrounding the show grounds at Thirty-Third Street and Seawall Boulevard, so the show could go on rain or shine.

Cody's announcement that this would be his last tour before he retired caused great excitement, and Galvestonians rushed to Star Drug Store to

Western show performers, including Texas Jack and Buffalo Bill (*back center, left and right*). *McCracken Research Library, Buffalo Bill Center of the West, Cody, Wyoming.*

purchase their one-dollar tickets. People from Hitchcock and other mainland communities traveled by train to attend the show, joining the thousands in the stands.

Cody appeared on the grounds in an embroidered buckskin shirt and broad-brimmed slouch hat, riding a horse with a silver-studded bridle and silver-embossed saddle. The cheers were said to be audible across the island. He was followed by a show filled with skilled horsemen, a reenacted Deadwood stagecoach robbery, the "reckless Cossack" Russian riders, Native Americans with face paint performing a war dance, Arabian acrobats, a troop of uniformed Mexican mounted police, "Crack Shot" Johnnie Baker (Cody's foster son) and other fast-paced entertainment.

At the end of the show, Bill removed his hat and made a grand bow before returning to his rooms at the Tremont.

Cody was destined to make one more trip to Galveston during an unexpected tour on October 25, 1915. Due to an unfortunate business deal, he was obligated to perform with the Sells-Floto Circus, which had gained rights to the Buffalo Bill Wild West Show. The production arrived over the causeway in thirty-nine railroad cars.

The showman led a mile-long parade through town with elephants, horses and performers in his wake traveling from Twenty-Seventh Street and Avenue N near the Garten Verein to Market Street, east to Twentieth Street, south to Postoffice Street, west to Tremont Street, south to Avenue M and west back to the circus tents at Twenty-Seventh Street and Avenue N.

Most of the circus personnel slept in the tent complex, but it is likely that Cody and other principals, for press reasons if nothing else, overnighted at the Tremont House.

It was Cody's last visit to Galveston.

# 10

# 1880 MARDI GRAS

The first Mardi Gras ball was held in the city founder Michel B. Menard's home in 1856, but the city's first official celebrations took place in 1871. Some of Galveston's most prominent citizens formed the Knights of Momus (known by the initials KOM) and Knights of Myth krewes, who rivaled each other to present the most elaborate costumes, parades and balls. People traveled from across the United States to witness and participate in the events, which were reported in the society pages of the *New York Times*.

The first few years of Mardi Gras on the island presented increasingly larger and more spectacular parades. But from the early 1880s until the early 1900s, the events scaled back, due to the mammoth expense of the spectacles, leaving the focus mainly on masked balls and private parties.

Even with fewer events and lower budgets, Galvestonians made the most of the celebrations, which is made evident by the lengths and humor involved in Momus's commencement of the season in 1880—entirely appropriate, since Momus was the Greek god of satire and mockery.

The *Daily News* reported the planned "arrival" in the city of the King of the Momus Krewe just as it would have narrated the presence of foreign dignitary, and the citizens of Galveston were more than happy to play along.

On Monday, February 9 local businesses, including the courthouse, banks, post office, port and other public offices, closed at 1:00 p.m. to allow employees to take part in the festivities, which centered on the Tremont House—known as Palace de Tremont for the occasion.

Captain Sweeny's tugboats *Inca* and *Index* and the U.S. revenue cutter *McLean* were re-dubbed as the day's royal fleet, all with festive bunting draped from their masts. They took King Momus and his court out into the bay to return to a grand reception.

His Majesty and his court were met with cannon fire and a grand ovation from onlookers as they docked and came ashore at Kuhn's Wharf at 2:30 p.m., where they were picked up by a "chariot and fleet of steeds."

Here they fell in line with a festive parade on Market Street, surrounded by excited onlookers who crowded the storefronts and leaned from windows to watch the spectacle.

The pageant included the Lone Star Band in their red uniforms and brass helmets; sheriff Captain Atkins and a police guard; the Washington Guards under the command of Captain Edmundson; an artillery company led by Captain Mott; Chief Dave Jordan and officers of the fire department followed by members of the fire department organized by company; engines and trucks of the fire department; King Momus and his court (who smiled and threw kisses to his adoring public); and a "royal escort" of fifteen uniformed horsemen.

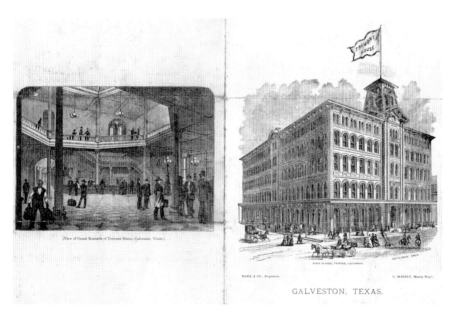

Front and back covers of illustrated Tremont House 1879 menu. *Galveston County Museum, Galveston, Texas.*

The entourage proceeded to the Tremont House, where the Ladies of the Dominion in full costume, along with a throng of visitors and locals, were waiting.

A signal was given from the "royal musicians," and the door of the Palace de Tremont opened to welcome King Momus, who slowly strolled to take a seat on a throne prepared in the center of the first floor of the rotunda.

Hundreds of onlookers around the second and third-floor balconies applauded and laughed as tongue-in-cheek speeches were made and a local alderman theatrically presented Momus with the golden keys to the city.

By 3:30 p.m., the event was over, and the court members retired to one of the Tremont's parlors to receive visitors, while younger attendees held an informal dance. All were invited to return at 8:00 p.m. when the cortege would march along another route to celebrate one of the last nights before Lent.

The happenings sound tame compared to contemporary festivities, but they were no less anticipated and enjoyed.

Each year at Mardi Gras, the Tremont decorated its entrance and rotunda for the carnival and sold tickets to local masked balls, many of which were held at Turner Hall.

# 11

# PRESIDENT ULYSSES S. GRANT

Former president Ulysses S. Grant, his family and traveling companions were thrilled to arrive at the Tremont House in 1880, not only because it was a grand hotel but also because their voyage to get there had been less than pleasant.

The group was returning to the United States from a trip to Mexico aboard the steamer *City of Mexico*, part of the fleet that belonged to the Alexandre steamship lines. Grant's arrival on the island was extensively covered in the national press due to speculation that he might decide to run for an unprecedented third term in the White House.

En route to Galveston, in response to an invitation extended the previous December by Leon Blum and 104 prominent Galvestonians, the steamer encountered a severe storm that delayed their arrival at the port. The lack of communication or sightings of the ship ignited rumors that it, along with its illustrious passengers, might have been lost.

Brief, panicked reports appeared across the nation, beginning with accounts of a Norwegian ship that had been dashed to pieces in the same gale, killing all aboard. Pleas for updates flooded into Galveston.

Grant's ship had been due in port on March 21, and as days passed beyond that date, worry increased. Samuel C. Vogt, a representative of the Alexandre steamship line, traveled to Galveston in the hope of greeting the belated arrival.

Portrait of Ulysses S. Grant (1822–1885). *Courtesy Library of Congress Prints and Photographs Division, Washington, D.C.*

A few ships arrived at the Galveston port on the morning of March 23 and shared harrowing tales about their experiences with the storm, which only heightened the general apprehension about the status of the *City of Mexico*.

Captain John Delaney, who had been scouting the horizon with his spyglass from the tower of Tremont House since dawn, finally caught sight of a steamer approaching from the west just after noon. Once it drew close enough to identify as the former president's ship, he shouted, "It's the *Mexico*, by George!" and raised the signal flag.

A recounting of the events in the next issue of the *News* noted that the most celebrated person in the city besides Grant was the man who climbed the pole of the flagstaff on the cupola of the Tremont in order to arrange the halyards to raise the flag.

At that signal, thousands of people filled the streets in anticipation of the arrival, and many found spots on balconies or roofs for improved views. An eager boy named Sweeny climbed to the roof of the Mallory Steamship Line building on the Strand but took a fall, breaking his nose and dislocating both arms.

The revenue cutter *Louis McLean* and Captain Irving's tugboat *Estelle* and steam lighter *S.F. Maddox* were immediately dispatched from the port to gather the travelers and bring them to shore. Each of the boats was filled with public figures yearning to be among the first to greet Grant. Though the *Estelle* was the last to leave the dock, its speed allowed it to pass the other two craft and arrive first at the *Mexico* at about two o'clock.

The continued swells made it unwieldy for the revenue cutter *McLean*, which was a side-wheel steamer, to come alongside the larger vessel, so it remained at a distance and allowed the thirty-foot-long, ten-foot-wide *Estelle* to receive the guests. Even after the boat was secured to the *Mexico*, safe transfer of Grant's party, especially the ladies, was a challenge but safely conducted with the assistance of those present.

General Grant; former first lady Julia Dent Grant; General Philip Sheridan; his wife, Irene; Grant's eldest son, Colonel Frederick Dent Grant; his wife, Ida; and other members of their party stood on the prow of the ship as it headed toward Galveston.

The eight additional passengers onboard, along with the remainder of the luggage, were transferred to the *Maddox*.

As the tugs pulled away from the steamship, the *Mexico* fired a single salute, and Grant waved goodbye to the crew who had brought them through the storm.

He then turned his attention to the welcoming party aboard the *Estelle*, which included his friend General Edward Otho Cresap Ord. There would not have been much time for the two to visit at that moment, as he was accompanied by a number of others, such as Colonel Vincent, adjutant general; Dr. Ashbel Smith, medical director; and Colonel Mansfield of the engineering department, who was stationed in Galveston at that time; along with railway officials, steamship agents and newspapermen.

Other boats in port flew welcome flags, and tugs sounded their horns in greeting as the crowd on shore gave rounds of resounding cheers.

Newspapermen aboard the tug took the opportunity to ask the arriving general questions, which he graciously accommodated. He made the remark to one of the reporters that this was his first visit to Galveston, but he would later correct himself at a speech at the Tremont House that it was a return visit.

Having been out of contact during the journey, the general was surprised when a reporter told him about the numerous telegrams asking if his ship had been lost at sea. When informed that the *New York Sun*, which had been particularly critical of him in the past, was especially anxious for updates, Grant laughed, "I expect the *Sun* will be sadly disappointed."

The rough weather had taken a toll on the passengers, who were anxious to step foot on solid ground. Ladies of the group especially seemed to be suffering from seasickness, and one shared her determination to "never, never go to sea again."

Grant's party drew ashore at the Williams-McKinney Wharf at the foot of Twenty-Fourth Street at 3:10 p.m. and were immediately welcomed—and most likely startled—by a "national salute" of artillery fire by a group under the command of Captain Marcus F. Mott.

After thirteen days on the steamship, they had finally arrived on dry land.

Police had cordoned off the eastern end of the wharf and put a police guard in place to protect the distinguished guests. Once escorted behind the ropes, Mayor Charles Leonard gave a brief speech, but it is doubtful much could be heard above the excitement of the crowd.

Bunting and flags were draped from every major building on the island.

After the harrowing voyage, the travelers most likely wanted nothing more than to go directly to the hotel to bathe and rest, but Galveston had orchestrated a series of grand welcomes. The weary visitors found themselves in the midst of an impending parade and were escorted into carriages along with Leonard and General Ord. The procession was led

*Top*: P.H. Rose Stereoview of view from Tremont House tower looking south. *Galveston Texas History Center of the Rosenberg Library, Galveston, Texas.*

*Bottom*: P.H. Rose Stereoview of view from Tremont House tower looking east. *Galveston Texas History Center of the Rosenberg Library, Galveston, Texas.*

by uniformed police, the Galveston Artillery, Washington Guards and a German brass band.

Moving slowly through muddy, rain-soaked streets, the convoy traveled up Twenty-Fourth Street beneath a banner that proclaimed "Welcome to the Island City" to the Strand, where Grant's carriage momentarily paused to allow him the opportunity to review the assembled units of firemen. The firemen then joined the procession at the back of the line as it continued down Twenty-Fourth Street to Broadway, took Broadway to Twentieth Street, continued on Twentieth Street to Market Street, up Market to Twenty-Second Street, down Twenty-Second to Church Street and finally up Church Street to the Tremont Hotel.

Along the way, parade participants grew to include the Lincoln Guards (an African American company); the United Brothers of Friendship and Sisters of the Mysterious Ten, Rising Sons of Progress and the Sons of Jerusalem (African American benevolent societies); and an African American cadet band.

The group arrived at their destination to find the street in front of the hotel teeming with people. Police took charge of clearing a path for the guests, mayor, alderman and the rest of the party to enter beneath a streamer painted with the words "We are all a band of brothers."

When they passed through the front doors, they found the rotunda nearly as crowded, with admirers filling the balconies on every level. The Lone Star Band, Galveston Artillery and Washington Guards entered first and, presenting arms, formed two lines that acted as a barricaded path to the stairway allowing the visitors to ascend to the second floor. As the party moved through the crowd, three cheers were sent up for the distinguished general.

The former president was led to a parlor to receive visitors, and the guards were dismissed. Firemen, the Lincoln Guards and African American societies were admitted first to greet the guest of honor, and then others were welcomed in a single column. Grant pleasantly spoke with numerous men and ladies, patted a baby's head and shook the hand of an elderly woman who was formerly enslaved.

At six o'clock, he and his companions were ushered into the dining room for dinner, and the doors were closed. A crowd lingered in the corridors hoping to catch a glimpse of the famous visitor but eventually dispersed.

The following day was scheduled full of activities and events.

Leonard invited the visitors to join him for a carriage ride at eleven o'clock for a morning drive along the beach and through some of Galveston's most attractive neighborhoods.

Upon returning to the Tremont, the ladies excused themselves, and Grant, Leonard and the men of the group embarked on an hour-long walk to visit other locations, including the *News* office and a Jewish synagogue.

When they arrived at the synagogue, the wedding of M. Freiberg and Nora Eldridge was taking place. Grant remained until after the ceremony to be introduced to Rabbi A. Blum and members of the congregation.

The Ladies' Reception given in honor of Julia Dent Grant, Irene Sheridan, Grant's daughter-in-law Ida Grant, Emma L. Courtney and other ladies of the party was given from three until five o'clock in the afternoon in the parlors of the Tremont. Though the gentlemen were also present, this was an opportunity to lavish attention on the women. A large number of Galveston ladies came to pay their respects and welcome them to the city.

Generals Grant and Ord took the opportunity after the reception to stroll through the business district of the city. Upon his return to the hotel, the honoree was greeted with a loud cheer by a crowd gathered outside, which he acknowledged by removing his hat and giving an elaborate bow.

The Grand Banquet for the honorees began at eight o'clock that night, and guests arrived to see the spacious dining hall delightfully decorated.

An extravagant menu was offered, comprising oysters on shell, Haute Sauterne, terrapin amontillado soup, sherry, fillet of trout a tartare, potato croquette en surprise, claret, boned turkey, prairie chicken, asparagus, quail, duck and more. The dessert offerings were equally elaborate presentations of pyramids of candied oranges, macaroons, meringue kisses, Mumm's extra dry champagne, Charlotte Russe, assorted cakes, vanilla ice cream, bananas, various fruits and black coffee.

Grant and Leonard were seated at a table at the south end of the room with Sheridan, Judge William Pitt Ballinger, Major Mansfied of the U.S. Engineers, Colonel Frederick Grant, General Ord, General B.C. Card, General Vincent, Dr. Ashbel Smith and H.C. Pratt, secretary of the committee of reception.

Among other guests present were J.S. Brown, A. Frank French, J.M. Brown, Colonel William Lewis Moody, O.G. Murray, former mayor and state legislator General Joseph Bates, Byron Andrews from the *Chicago Inter-Ocean* newspaper, W.J. Hutchings, legislator Henry Jacob Labatt, H.T. Sloan, George Sealy, Moritz Kopperl, Dr. John M. Haden, Charles Vidor, Ben Blum and Julius Runge.

At the end of the meal, Leonard stood to speak and joked, "We have been for a great many years trying to capture General Grant and not able to do it, but at last he has come to us and surrendered himself a prisoner." The remark was met with applause and laughter.

P.H. Rose Stereoview of view from Tremont House tower looking northeast. *Galveston Texas History Center of the Rosenberg Library, Galveston, Texas.*

Grant responded with a gracious speech of his own, followed by Sheridan, who stated that the improvement of Galveston "probably can be well illustrated by simply referring to this magnificent hotel that we are in here tonight."

Speeches and toasts continued into the late hours, often mentioning the hospitality of Tremont House.

Thursday's planned activities included a reception at the cotton press and Cotton Exchange, after which Grant rode with Colonel William H. Sinclair to visit the Barnes Institute Avenue M near Twenty-Ninth Street.

The school had been founded ten years earlier by missionary Sarah Barnes to educate the formerly enslaved and train teachers. The welcome speech was given by student Willie Whales, who respectfully referred to the fact that Grant's photo hung in the school.

The general responded, "Teachers and children, I am very glad to meet you, and hope that you will become good citizens and educated men and women. I am glad to see that the colored children of Galveston have the opportunity of becoming useful citizens, and hope that you will improve it by obtaining a common school education and that the white children will do likewise. If you do not improve the opportunity it is your own fault. Allow me to thank you for your kind reception and the attention you have given me."

The day's events finished with a redfish chowder social at Garten Verein at four o'clock, for which tickets were issued.

That evening, Grant penned a letter on Tremont House stationery to one of his most ardent supporters, Elihu B. Washburne, responding to a request for a statement about his intention to run for a third term of office. He stated that there were others he would prefer to have the office, but he would accept a nomination under the right circumstances.

Grant did attempt to gain the nomination but failed and passed away from throat cancer five years later.

# 12

# ACTOR EDWIN BOOTH

Galveston's prosperity in the 1880s manifested in many ways, including exquisite theaters that attracted major talent. The famous Shakespearean thespian Edwin Booth was among them.

Though the name Booth conjures images of a presidential assassination, before John Wilkes Booth became an assassin, he was a well-known stage actor. He remains a notorious figure in history but at the time was not as famous or respected as his brother Edwin Booth.

The brothers became estranged at the onset of the Civil War, with John siding with the Secessionists and Edward being a devout Unionist. Ironically, months before John shot President Abraham Lincoln in 1865, Edwin had saved the life of Robert Todd Lincoln, the president's son, in a train station incident.

Edwin Booth appeared on the Galveston stage at the Tremont Opera House for the first time in a production running from January 24 to 28, 1882. He, his daughter Edwina Booth and the performing company's manager, Maze Edwards, stayed at the Tremont House, while lesser-known actors most likely were housed at less expensive establishments.

Their advance ticket agent arrived on the island on January 8 to arrange for sales and advertising, and from that day forward the newspapers and gathering places of Galveston were abuzz with excitement about the opportunity to see the great actor. The *News* reported that the city was "full of strangers attracted hither by the presence of Edwin Booth." Only a lucky few were able to obtain rooms at the Tremont in order to chance an encounter with the famous tragedian offstage.

*Right*: Portrait of actor Edwin Booth (1833–1893). *Courtesy Library of Congress Prints and Photographs Division, Washington, D.C.*

*Below*: Verkin Studio photo of Tremont Hotel, circa 1925. *Galveston Texas History Center of the Rosenberg Library, Galveston, Texas.*

An audience of 1,400 admirers packed the opera house and were treated to performances of *The Merchant of Venice*, *Othello* and *The Quiet Family*. The forty-nine-year-old actor received glowing reviews—much more so than his fellow performers. General admission to the show ranged from $0.50 to $1.00 and $1.50; tickets in the parquette and parquette circle were $2.00; and the dress circle seats were $1.50. A rousing success, the engagement earned ticket sales over $8,600.

On their last full day in Galveston, Booth and Edwina assisted the touring company's manager, who hosted a private picnic on the beach for the ladies and gentlemen of the cast. Lunch, prepared by the kitchen staff of the Tremont, was served, and music, singing and dancing were enjoyed on the sand. Reporters were not permitted to approach the party and were relegated to observing from afar. After the picnic, the ladies in the group were treated to dray rides along the waterfront.

Booth returned to the island for successful engagements in February 1887 and February 1888 but by then was traveling and staying in private railroad cars, only taking meetings and occasional interviews at the Tremont House.

13

# 1885 EXPLOSION

Sunday morning, May 3, 1885, had begun with quiet daily routines at the Tremont. At that time, in addition to guests, there was a wide range of full-time residents at the hotel, including all stations of society ranging from employees of the hotel to the consul for France.

Hotel manager Henry Weaver went to the engine and boiler room to make sure all hands were busily at work. The room was a one-story brick structure attached to the rear of the west wing of the hotel (at the northwest corner), next to Twenty-Fourth Street. It was equipped with two fifty-horsepower boilers, installed the previous October, and machinery necessary for running the kitchen, laundry, elevator and other departments of the hotel.

Only one of the large twelve-foot tubular boilers was being used at the time. The hotel's practice was to alternate use of their two boilers each week. That morning one was cooling down and finishing its cycle, and the one the men were attending was almost at full steam, registering fifty pounds of pressure.

Seeing that each man was tending to the machinery, Weaver returned to his family quarters at the hotel to read the newspaper.

Robert Carter, employed as a cleaner, stopped into the engine room as well and witnessed engineer Thomas Cross "rubbing the water glass" and fireman Larry Carr sitting on top of the boiler cleaning the safety valve with a rag. He noticed a jagged, patched hole in the boiler, which he remembered had resulted from a repaired crack a few months prior.

After talking with the men for a few moments Carter returned to the hotel, passing bellboy John Axman, who was on his way to the engine room to turn on steam pressure for the elevator just before 7:30 a.m.

Within minutes after the visits, a terrible explosion shook the hotel and surrounding buildings, shattering windows in the area and sending debris flying.

Weaver gathered his family and rushed them out of their rooms. Other guests, in all states of getting dressed, made hasty exits, shouting in a general panic.

The two boilers had been arranged parallel running east and west, and the unused boiler was thrown sideways into the alley from the force of the explosion. It aided in the obliteration of the brick walls of the engineering room. Cross and Carr were killed instantly.

Brick, immense pieces of timber, shattered furniture, bedding and even human bodies were propelled into the air as witnesses were stunned by the initial blast and then terrified by the rumbling sounds of falling brick, crashing timber and other damage in the wake of the propelled boiler. The

Riders on horseback outside of Tremont House. *Galveston County Museum, Galveston Texas.*

few people who were on the streets in the vicinity at that early hour had to scatter for cover from falling debris.

The heated boiler was thrown westward, crashing through the northern end of a long two-story frame building used as apartments by hotel staff, and a span of a rafter went through the roof of a building on Church Street just opposite the hotel.

The east end of the boiler burst through the wall of the main building into the laundry room and tore away a large section of the brick. It passed through the second story of this building, which fronted Church Street at Twenty-Fourth and joined to the back end of the Lone Star Stable owned by Lovell J. Bartlett. Anderson Jones, an African American employee of the stables, was killed instantly. His mangled body was thrown across Twenty-Fourth Street fifty feet into the alley on the other side, where it remained for some time in the aftermath of the disaster. The twenty-eight-year-old victim was later identified by his brother Henry.

The boiler continued its flight, smashing the chimneys of Fred Smith's blacksmith shop on the alley corner; tearing off the roof and one side of Mr. Flemming's cottage, home of Rose Montgomery; and destroying an adjoining stable.

Asleep in her house behind the Tremont, Montgomery survived without injury, crawling from beneath the ruins of the cottage.

The projectile continued its path and demolished a small house of prostitution occupied and operated by an African American woman named Julia Winters. The building was torn apart, but Winters and all of her working women escaped serious harm, including Lucy Turner, whose arm was badly bruised.

Two other residents in the house were not as lucky. Eighteen-year-old Clara Miller, a Caucasian woman also known as Clara Kuntz, and her twenty-five-year-old companion, newspaperman Morris "Yank" Sullivan, were badly injured either by flying timbers or pieces of the boiler itself which had scattered debris around the scene.

Miller and Sullivan were taken immediately to the hospital, but the woman perished from her injuries on the way. Her body was taken to Crossman & Simpson's undertaking business on Postoffice, where a temporary morgue had been arranged to receive bodies as they were recovered from the debris. That establishment had also been damaged during the explosion, having its rear doors blown off and roof damaged from falling brick.

A fifteen-pound piece of iron crashed through the roof of William Ruhl's blacksmith shop on Market Street.

What remained of the deadly boiler had traveled nearly four hundred feet from its origin, tearing a hole in Samuel Johnson's saddlery, and came to rest positioned half inside and half outside a house on Bath Avenue, now named Rosenberg Avenue.

Witnesses were shocked at the amount of damage, found as far away as Twenty-Seventh Street, that had occurred within minutes. The glass had shattered in surrounding buildings, and a chaotic jumble of boiler iron, pipes and splintered timber littered the streets. A curious few who tried to pick up pieces of the still scalding-hot iron were badly burned.

Fire engines arrived at the scene to ensure no fires erupted in the ruins, and police cordoned off unstable areas to prevent further injuries as the search for victims began. The north end of the west wall above the explosion site at the rear of the Tremont was particularly precarious, as a large, unstable brick chimney towered above.

Several onlookers fainted on viewing the devastation.

Badly disfigured remains of forty-eight-year-old Cross, the engineer, were identified by his inconsolable wife, Mary, as he was pulled from a pile of brick and debris near where the boiler once stood. The couple had several children.

A group of people at the Girardin House on Market Street witnessed the body of twenty-six-year-old Carr, the fireman, being tossed over one wing of the five-story hotel by the explosion. It then fell into an inner court wall and through the tin roof of the pump house. His feet were later retrieved separately on Church and Twenty-Fourth Streets. The New Orleans native left a wife and two children.

The four recovered victims were placed in pine board coffins and laid side by side at the undertakers, as Justice Spann began an inquest. Though the scene at the morgue was a solemn one as relatives and coworkers came to make final identifications, morbid curiosity-seekers gathered about the area to view the scene of the explosion and see the bodies.

Louis Marx, manager of the Tremont House cigar store, instituted a drive for funds to aid the destitute Mrs. Carr and her children. As she was unable to pay for her husband's funeral, his remains were buried by county authorities.

Injured victims taken to the hospital included R. Waldin, an African American waiter at the hotel who had been sitting in a kitchen window shelling green peas when the explosion occurred. Debris from the force inflicted a compound fracture to his neck and multiple lacerations on his head.

Sullivan, who had been at Winter's house, was considered in critical condition suffering a brain concussion but survived. Lucky to have narrowly escaped, the bellboy Axman, who had visited the boiler room just before the occurrence, was treated for a fractured collarbone and cuts on his head and body. One of the laundry women, Mrs. Burns, was hospitalized with bruises on her head and arms, and head baker and pastry cook Jose Aguillo was badly scaled and received internal injuries.

Immediately after being notified of the accident, George McGinley, superintendent of the Tremont and Grand Windsor Hotel Company in Dallas, which owned the hotel, took the first train from Houston and arrived on the scene by noon. The company, owned by Colonel W.E. Hughes of Dallas, operated the Grand Windsor Hotel in Dallas, the Capitol Hotel in Houston and the Tremont in Galveston.

Hughes arrived from Dallas two days after the tragedy to assess the damage to the Tremont, which was estimated to be $15,000. A large number of men were already at work clearing away the debris and making preparations for repairs, and police were kept busy keeping curious passersby away from the scene. A temporary boiler had been secured to provide power for the laundry and kitchen, and only the elevator was still out of service.

A lengthy inquest into the cause of the explosion was strewn with unfounded theories, including an accusation by a representative of the boiler's manufacturer that incompetence caused the accident. That idea was soon dismissed, as a series of witnesses testified to the engineer's reliability and experience.

Though the general consensus was that the boiler itself was defective, proof could not be agreed upon. It was concluded that the cause of the explosion could not be determined.

Work proceeded on repairing the Tremont House, and within weeks the headlines had left the story of the tragedy behind.

14

# AUTHOR STEPHEN CRANE

By the time twenty-three-year-old Stephen Crane arrived at the Tremont House in Galveston in March 1895, he was already known for his war correspondence, short stories, articles and a novel titled *Maggie: A Girl of the Streets*. Though a shortened version of his story *Red Badge of Courage* had appeared in serialized form in newspapers the previous year, it would not be released as a novel until the following November.

Just days before his arrival, his features about travel to Nebraska and Hot Springs, Arkansas, part of a series of articles about his tour of the West and Mexico he was writing for a newspaper syndicate, had been published locally. His visit to Galveston, in between stops at New Orleans and San Antonio, was an opportunity to gather material for the same assignment.

He later wrote of the arrival of his train as it approached the island, "by means of a long steel bridge across a bay, which glitters like burnished metal in the wintertime sunlight."

James Henry Moser, an artist friend of Crane's, recommended he contact his acquaintance Samuel Moore Penland to make introductions. Penland was a nephew of General Sam Houston and well-connected in the city. Fifty-year-old Penland was a childless widower who lived one and a half blocks from the Tremont and took his meals there. It was arranged for him to meet Crane upon his arrival at the hotel.

In a letter written on Tremont stationery to Moser on March 6, Crane described Galveston as "square blocks of brick businesses with mazes of telegraph wires and trolley cars clamoring up and down the streets."

He called Penland a "peach" and detailed the humorous "drinking bouts" that resulted from local officials who unknowingly made separate attempts to entertain the journalist.

Mayor Dr. Ashley W. Fly greeted the writer at ten o'clock in the morning, hardly an hour after his arrival. They spent the afternoon touring the island by automobile, during which time he wrote, "We drank more cocktails than I ever saw in my whole lifetime before. I was near dead from it."

He parted company with the mayor in the late afternoon to get work accomplished with Clarence Ousley, the managing editor of the *Galveston Daily News*.

The editor began their meeting by declaring, "Mr. Crane, I don't know your habits but as for me I always like to get up to concert pitch before I begin work."

Portrait of author
Stephen Crane
(1871–1900).
*Author's collection.*

Main lobby area of Tremont House. *Galveston Texas History Center of the Rosenberg Library, Galveston, Texas.*

"So we drank up to concert pitch," Crane's letter continued.

When their meeting was over, Crane excused himself to attend the theater with the mayor, who greeted him by saying, "Well, let's go over to the club and get a drink,"

"My struggle through that day was a distinctly Homeric one," Crane wrote. "To my honor be it said that I didn't mention the managing editor to the mayor nor the mayor to the managing editor, but withstood both assaults with good manners and tranquility. If any man hereafter says I can't hold liquor, he lies."

The club Fly escorted Crane to was the Aziola Club near Tremont House, a members-only gentleman's club frequented by influential men in the business community. Its charter stated it had been formed "for the purpose of establishing and maintaining a reading room, the promotion of painting, music, and other fine arts, and the cultivation of social intercourse."

Besides a dining room, the club maintained two large lounging areas, a billiard room, two small game rooms and, of course, a bar.

Honorary memberships to the Aziola Club were often extended to esteemed visitors and sometimes even those who never stepped across the threshold, such as Thomas Edison. Crane received a formal letter of invitation to membership within weeks of his stay on the island.

Despite the amount of alcohol Crane encountered on his trip, he seems to have left with a favorable impression, as his letter ended, "Galveston is a great town I think, and all heavy wit aside I am deeply indebted to you for introducing me to such a royal good fellow as Sam Penland."

Stephen Crane died at the age of twenty-eight on June 5, 1900. His article about Galveston, which he portrayed as both a seaport and resort, was published posthumously the following November when interest in the island increased due to the 1900 Storm.

# 15

# A FLOATING COFFIN

Though many actors and performers resided at the Tremont House while visiting the island, there is only one whose story later appeared in *Ripley's Believe It or Not*, a national newspaper panel that highlighted bizarre and unusual places and occurrences.

The story began when a young stage actor named Charles Francis Coghlan visited a "gypsy" fortune-teller on a whim. The mysterious woman told Coghlan that he would perish in a southern city at the height of his fame. To make matters worse, she added that he would not rest in peace until his body was returned home.

In the following years, Coghlan shared the prediction with family and friends, confiding that the notion haunted him.

Over the next thirty years, Coghlan became one of the most famous actors of the day, appearing on stages across the United States and Europe. During the rare weeks that he did not appear on stage, he and his wife retreated to their beloved home on Canada's Prince Edward Island.

On October 30, 1899, Coghlan arrived in Galveston with his performing troupe, ready to present one of his own works, titled *The Royal Box*. He never had the chance to appear on the Galveston stage in this production, however. He became seriously ill with what doctors at the time diagnosed as acute gastritis. His understudy, Mr. Robinson, received wonderful reviews, often mistakenly credited to Coghlan in print.

The actor's wife remained with him, transcribing the first four acts of a new play for his daughter named *Vanity Fair*, which he dictated while resting for four weeks. But after an abrupt relapse of pain, he died in bed at the Tremont House on November 27, with his distraught wife by his side. He was fifty-seven years old and at the peak of his career.

Coghlan's body was taken to the Levy Brothers' Funeral Home until his wife could manage arrangements following Coghlan's wishes. He had requested to be cremated, but there was no crematorium in Galveston at the time. The grieving widow, who struggled to make difficult decisions without the support of family, made plans to have her husband's remains shipped to a crematorium in St. Louis and then to New York City, where he wanted to be buried.

As news about the beloved actor's demise was reported in papers across the country, however, family members and ardent fans began to send demands that things be handled differently. In the confusion, the flustered

Actor Charles Francis Coghlan (1842–1899).
*Courtesy Library of Congress Prints and Photographs Division, Washington, D.C.*

widow, who had run out of money, had Coghlan placed in the granite receiving vault at Lakeview Cemetery until she could raise the funds to have him taken to the East Coast in the following months.

Time dragged on, and Coghlan remained in his temporary resting place until fate stepped in.

In September 1900, a devastating hurricane struck the island, killing thousands of people. Coghlan's was one of a number of caskets that were swept out of mausoleums and vaults by the storm surge. Though many were found and reinterred in the cemeteries, the actor's coffin was never recovered.

It was believed that his casket, along with the bodies of many storm victims, was caught in the swift-running current and taken out into the Gulf of Mexico. The New York Actor's Club offered a sizable reward for its return, but it was never located. Because his widow had purchased an elaborate cast-iron casket for her beloved, it is highly unlikely it could do anything but sink in a body of water.

In 1929, an edition of *Ripley's Believe It or Not* published a rumor that had developed in the years after the storm. The original fantastical feature stated: "Charles Coghlan comes home! He died in 1899, and he was buried in Galveston. When the tragic flood came his coffin was washed out to sea and the Gulf Stream carried him around Florida and up the coast to Prince Edward Island—2,000 miles distant—where he had lived."

Ripley claimed that in October 1908 (eight years after the hurricane), fishermen spied a large box floating in the Gulf of St. Lawrence. Snagging it with their nets, they pulled the badly damaged object to shore. A silver plate was revealed after cleaning off a few barnacles, identifying it as the casket of Charles Coghlan.

The tabloid-style account stated that the actor was then taken to his home church on Prince Edward Island and buried near the church where he was baptized in 1841. His wandering spirit was finally home.

The tale has become an urban myth, and numerous books and articles have been written about the incident over the years, with slight to outrageous changes in the details. A brief internet search yields several versions of the story.

Local cemetery records of the small church on Prince Edward are considered complete and accurate. They show no sign of Charles Coghlan's burial, and no gravestone exists.

It was also reported that his daughter, actress Gertrude Coghlan Pitou, visited Prince Edward in the 1980s and stated that her father's remains had not been recovered or reinterred in Galveston or elsewhere. This report is seemingly eerie enough, since Gertrude died in 1952.

His sister, actress Rose Coghlan, was highly offended by the stories about her brother, and she asked Robert Ripley for a retraction. Ripley, ever the savvy businessman, declined. He credited Sir Johnston Forbes Robertson, a Shakespearean actor and friend of Coghlan, for sharing the story with the publication.

The mystery of what became of Coghlan and his cast-iron casket is doomed to remain unsolved.

Five years after the loss of her brother, Rose Coghlan performed on the Galveston stage, staying at the same hotel where he passed away.

# 16

# 1900 STORM

The event known as the 1900 Storm was a Category 4 hurricane that struck Galveston, Texas, on September 8, 1900, killing between six and twelve thousand of the island's forty-two thousand inhabitants. It remains the deadliest natural disaster in U.S. history.

At the time of the storm, the highest point in the city of Galveston was less than seven feet above sea level. The hurricane brought a storm surge of over fifteen feet, overtaking the island.

The Tremont House played a pivotal role in saving hundreds of lives during the tragedy and provided a gathering place for recovery in the aftermath.

On the afternoon of September 8, 1900, Morris Sheppard concentrated on writing a speech in his room at the Tremont House. As the sovereign banker of the Woodmen of the World fraternal society, he was scheduled to deliver the address at a meeting that night. The young man, who would later serve a total of thirty-eight years as a U.S. representative and senator from Texas, was accompanied on the trip by the Woodmen's Sovereign Commander W.A. Fraser.

Once Sheppard's writing was finished, he and Fraser adjourned to the downstairs dining room for a midafternoon meal. It would be the last proper meal served at the hotel for days.

Tremont House had approximately two hundred paying guests registered, and many of them were wandering the lobby, excitedly visiting with each other about the "big blow" of a storm they heard was coming to the island.

Despite the strong northerly breeze, most Galvestonians went through their day as if nothing unusual was expected, and the downtown area was filled with businessmen and shoppers.

As the rain began, the streets quickly filled with twelve inches of water, which was not considered unusual taking into account the low elevation of the island and that high curbs of the business district held water in the roadways.

Horse-drawn vehicles had increasing difficulty navigating through the water, but their drivers persisted. The Tremont Hotel's immense fifteen-passenger conveyance arrived at the Santa Fe Depot to retrieve the first morning's passengers as usual, but by the time it made the trip to meet the last train from the mainland, the water was up to the horses' stomachs.

By four o'clock, several families had made their way to the Tremont from residential districts.

The hotel did not serve supper that night.

One visitor later recalled, "I was in a restaurant near the Tremont Hotel when the storm broke. It began blowing a gale about two o'clock in the afternoon, but the wind did not reach an alarming height until about four. Myself and my friends saw that it was going to be a storm of more than ordinary fury and started for the Tremont. The street was three feet deep in water and we got a carriage. We had to draw our feet up on the seats to keep out of the water."

Harry Van Easton, a traveling salesman for Tennison Brothers in Dallas, had arrived in Galveston that morning and noted the persistent wind and rain but was so unconcerned that he and his friends started toward the beach to see the storm arrive. They were soon taken off guard by the rate the water was rising and quickly attempted to return to the Tremont.

"Before we reached it," he later recalled, "we had to wade in water waist-deep. Within a few minutes, women and children began to flock to the hotel for refuge. All were panic-stricken. I saw two women, one with a child, trying to get to the hotel. They were drowned not 300 yards from us."

Another Saturday morning arrival had immediately gone to the beach with friends to enjoy surf bathing. As waves became increasingly violent, lifesaving crews warned them of danger, and they hurriedly exited the water. By the time they dressed to return to the hotel, they too faced wading through waist-deep water before reaching the Tremont.

Even with its position at a high point on the island, the hotel was not safe from the rising waters, and by five o'clock it had risen over the front sidewalks.

Salesman Walter Davis worried that he should have returned to his hotel room earlier when he found himself wading down Tremont Street, dodging rowboats carrying people attempting to reach Tremont House.

The previously jovial anticipation of people inside the hotel concerning the storm turned into morbid curiosity and then shock as injured men, women and children were carried inside or staggered by themselves through the doors before they collapsed in exhaustion.

People for blocks around struggled against the winds and rushing water full of telegraph poles, boxes, wood, kegs, and other debris. Flying items made deadly by the force they were blown—including broken glass, metal and roof slates—added to the peril.

Any who were able to reach the sidewalk outside of Tremont House were pulled inside to safety. As the storm raged, the number of refugees increased to about one thousand people. That number eclipsed the two hundred hotel guests.

At 5:30 p.m., water poured over the porch, through the doors and across the marble floor. As the rotunda flooded, those on the first floor were forced to retreat upstairs. Increasing winds shook the large structure, which

Illustration of 1900 Storm outside of the Tremont Hotel. *Galveston Texas History Center of the Rosenberg Library, Galveston, Texas.*

vibrated, as one railroad man sheltering within later described it, "not unlike that of a boxcar in motion."

By that time, refugees, who had been arriving for hours, ceased to appear in the doorway, as movement outside was impossible.

Windows shattered, and guests who had sheltered inside their rooms rushed into the corridors to join others huddled in the hallways and on staircases.

Forceful winds struck at around six o'clock in the evening. The skylight exploded and sent rain and shards of glass into the rotunda. Part of the roof over the office blew away, and the servants' quarters at the rear of the building shattered.

Thankfully, the remainder of the roof held and kept those inside safe from further harm. A lucky few found dry matches and bits of candles, which they occasionally lit to relieve the darkness.

The wet, crowded galleries and stairwells were filled with frightened locals and visitors, some of whose clothing had been torn off by the force of the water. As the wind howled outside, hotel manager George Korst did everything in his power to help the guests and refugees, but his control of the situation was obviously limited. Those who attempted rest, even though exhausted, were kept awake by the bedlam of buildings crashing around them.

The brunt of the storm hit around eight o'clock as hundreds of frantic people pressed against each other in the dark. Screams rang out at the crashing sound of a falling smokestack that destroyed the engine house of the hotel. Witnesses later remembered that bricks were thrown with enough force to fly parallel to the ground.

Water continued to rise until it reached three and a half feet in the lobby around 9:30 p.m., covering the front desk and its papers. The depth of the water outside of the Tremont was seven feet.

As midnight approached, conditions became worse, and the terrified refugees said their preemptive goodbyes to one another, prayed and sang hymns. One woman, said to have been a madam from one of the local houses of prostitution, lost her senses and reportedly threw $10,000 worth of diamonds into the floodwaters—perhaps in an attempt to appease them.

Men and women alike fainted under the stress, and winds and water rose in the pitch-black hotel until about 1:45 a.m. on Sunday.

Within hours, the storm began to quiet, and by five o'clock in the morning, the water had receded from the hotel, leaving a foot of mud and sand.

Daylight did not bring relief, as the reality of the tragedy dawned on the city and survivors roamed the streets searching for loved ones. Stunned people began to form a crowd around the Tremont, which opened its upper floors to anyone who needed refuge until no space was left.

The Tremont kitchen served breakfast to the fortunate few who could pay four dollars for all they could salvage to provide: a small piece of bacon and a cup of coffee.

In the aftermath of the storm, inventor Thomas Edison sent crews with his version of the newfangled moving picture camera to capture scenes of the devastation. The clips, less than one minute long each, include one taken of the Tremont House still standing after the tragedy. The films are now housed at the Library of Congress.

Traveling salesman Charles Law, who survived the storm at the Tremont, wrote a ten-page letter to his wife in Marietta, Georgia, recounting his experiences. The missive was written partially on Tremont House stationery and partially on paper from Houston's Capital Hotel, where he retreated in

Gathering the storm dead on Tremont Street. *Galveston Texas History Center of the Rosenberg Library, Galveston, Texas.*

the following days. The sometimes graphically gruesome story he wrote has remained in the Law family since 1900.

In addition to details of the storm itself, he commented on the oppressive heat the following day and how his sample trunks had floated in the office and were then too rain-soaked to bring back with him.

The chamber of commerce, which regularly met at the Tremont House, returned to the hotel to organize a Central Relief Committee and subcommittees.

Clara Barton and her staff from the Red Cross reached Galveston within days of the hurricane and set up relief headquarters at Tremont House.

Galveston congressman Robert Bradley Hawley returned from Washington on September 12 to give a speech in the Tremont rotunda to reassure citizens that the nation was aware of and sympathetic to their plight.

A Galveston Houston and Henderson Railroad steamer arrived at the foot of Tremont Street on Tuesday to take passengers to the mainland. Regular fare tickets, for those who could afford them, were available at the Tremont House ticket office.

Other passengers frantic to escape were shuttled by tugboats, rowboats and any method available.

On Thursday, September 13, a wedding took place at Tremont House. The sixteen-year-old bride, Elizabeth "Bessie" Roberts, was a saleslady at a clothing store. Her twenty-six-year-old groom, lawyer Ernest A. Mayo, was a candidate for prosecuting attorney. They had dated for several months, and both had suffered tragic losses in the storm. It was decided to face to future together, and they took their vows with no family, flowers or music. The couple left that day to live on Mayo's property in Dickinson.

Major Frank M. Spencer made his way to the island three days later with $50,000 cash from Governor Sayers, earmarked to aid in the disposal of debris and the burial of bodies. The bank was closed when he arrived, so it remained guarded by soldiers in the Tremont Hotel for twenty-four hours.

In the days, weeks and months following the 1900 Storm, lists of the dead were published in newspapers across the state, occasionally updated as bodies were found and mistakes discovered. Marcellus Elliot Foster, managing editor of the *Houston Post*, ingeniously published the names of some survivors instead, from registry lists being kept at Tremont House.

Within a month, an entrepreneurial Boston contractor named Robert J. Culbertson set up an office at the hotel to "cheerfully give estimates for all kinds of buildings and repair work."

Damage to the hotel amounted to $25,000, and once repairs were made, the Tremont resumed business as usual but with an even greater respect from the community.

# 17

# ANGEL IN THE AFTERMATH

Clarissa Harlowe Barton, better known as Clara Barton, was the founder of the American Red Cross and a heroine of Civil War battlefields.

Though at an advanced age for the trying task, she and her staff responded in person to the cry for help from Galveston victims after the 1900 Storm. With over six thousand killed and more than ten thousand homeless, there was much work to be done.

Word of the disaster reached Barton at her headquarters in Washington on Monday, September 10, and she and her committee of ten helpers immediately set out for Texas. They arrived in Texas City, across the water from Galveston, on September 13. There was no immediate means to transfer them across the water, so they remained there for twenty-four hours and slept on boards placed across the tops of railcar seats.

Texas City had also been hit by the storm, but Galveston victims were brought there a boatload at a time seeking help and medical attention.

At dark, a glow could be seen from the direction of Galveston, and the Barton group was informed that it was from funeral pyres rather than electric lights. Barton counted twenty-three pyres within sight from the distance and later noted that the air was filled with the horrid smell of burning flesh.

The next morning, Barton and her companions took a boat to the island, where they were met with unimaginable devastation. Refugees and victims wandered in a stupor amid what Barton described as

Portrait of Clara Barton (1821–
1912). *Courtesy Library of Congress
Prints and Photographs Division,
Washington, D.C.*

*the debris of broken houses, crushed to splinters and piled twenty feet high,
along miles of sea coast, where a space, six blocks wide, of the city itself
was gone, and seas rolled over populated avenues; heaps of splintered wood
were filled with furniture of once beautiful habitations—beds, pianos,
chairs, tables—all that made up happy homes. Worse than that the bodies
of the owners were rotting therein, twenty or thirty of them being taken out
every day as workmen removed the rubbish and laid it in great piles of ever-
burning fire, covering the corpses with mattresses, doors, boards—anything
that was found near them, and then left them to burn out or go away in
impregnated smoke, while the weary workmen toiled on the next.*

There was no time to waste.

The men of her committee set up living quarters in an intact warehouse
of the old Santa Fe Building at the corner of Twenty-Fifth Street and
the Strand, supplied by John Sealy. The women stayed at the Tremont,
which offered the only respectable accommodations on the island, despite
its damage.

On Sunday, September 16, the Central Relief Committee was overwhelmed with the tasks at hand, including burying the dead and clearing debris to allow for relief efforts. Brigadier General Thomas Scurry and two hundred Texas State Volunteer Guard men had arrived to put an end to looting, and his order that all able-bodied men should labor to the limit of their strength was carried out to the letter.

At Barton's first meeting with the local Central Relief Committee, her presence was offhandedly dismissed and she was told they did not need nurses. One of her spokesmen retorted that was fortunate because they had none to provide and asked what it was that they needed most.

Their answer was surgical dressings and medical supplies. Barton sent one telegraph, and a large order of the supplies arrived within twenty-four hours.

After that, officials who previously did not understand the power this special woman wielded took her very seriously.

Next, Barton sent out a plea for lumber, hardware and furnishings in the nation's newspapers and received a favorable response.

The Red Cross committee included Barton's nephew Stephen E. Barton, Red Cross vice president, and Fred L. Ward, its secretary, who organized departments to address specific needs such as stoves, heaters, food, clothing, bedding, blankets and other necessities.

The *New York World* newspaper instigated a fundraising campaign to aid victims in Galveston and announced that the funds would be turned over to Barton to be used for food, clothing and shelter.

A local women's Red Cross Society was established, as well as an African American auxiliary, to guarantee that supplies were distributed fairly. Their meetings were held at the Tremont and local church buildings.

Governor Joseph Draper Sayers dispatched Major Frank M. Spencer to Galveston with $50,000 cash to be used for the disposal of debris. Spencer arrived too late to deposit the money in a bank, so it remained in the Tremont House guarded by soldiers for twenty-four hours.

After long days filled with meetings and details, Barton found little rest at night.

She dictated sixty to eighty letters each day to her stenographer, Mary Agnes Coombs, which were taken to clerical offices each morning to be posted.

It is no wonder that seventy-eight-year-old Barton's health wavered under the conditions and strain of the tasks at hand.

On the morning of Tuesday, September 18, Barton held a staff meeting in her room at Tremont House to deliver detailed work assignments for each person. As she completed her presentation, she suddenly ceased to speak. She simply added, "Now I want to hear the views of my advisers."

She returned to her seat, leaned to Ellen Spencer Mussey, a member of her staff, and whispered, "Begin talking. I am about to faint. Don't let them see."

Mussey rose and stood in front of Barton, made a brief speech of encouragement and dismissed the attendees.

Galvestonian Dr. William Mercer, who had previously visited Barton, was called in but did not consider her to be in serious condition.

In the afternoon, her temperature rose to 102 degrees, and the doctor reported that she must leave the island immediately. The physician told her assistant that she might only live a few hours, but Barton overheard him and reassured the woman, "I shall not die. Don't let them frighten you."

Barton refused to leave her post, so she was tended by four nurses in her hotel room. She recuperated ten days later from what is thought to have been double pneumonia and returned to her relief work more determined than ever.

A notice appeared in the newspaper on September 27 stating the "American Red Cross, under the management of Miss Clara Barton, is now prepared to give a temporary home to orphan or destitute children in Galveston. Applications for admitting the children to the Red Cross Asylum are solicited at the headquarters of the Red Cross, corner of Strand and 25th."

The asylum would be created in the old Santa Fe Building, again thanks to the courtesy of Sealy.

Progress had been made, but the clearing of debris, funeral pyres and other heartbreaking tasks of the aftermath continued.

After two months, Barton made the decision to leave the island, leaving only two representatives to run the orphanage for two months until family, friends or other homes could be found for the children.

Barton received numerous visitors at the Tremont who were anxious to express thanks to her and her workers before their departure.

The night before she left Galveston, a reporter from the *Tribune* interviewed her and her nephew about their work on the island. Barton replied that she was happy about the way so many parties came together to help. "It is pleasing to feel that the regret at our departure is caused not so much at the thought of losing our aid, but as losing friends."

"This work is now so well organized and so far advanced," her nephew added, "that Miss Barton and her staff can retire without its suffering the

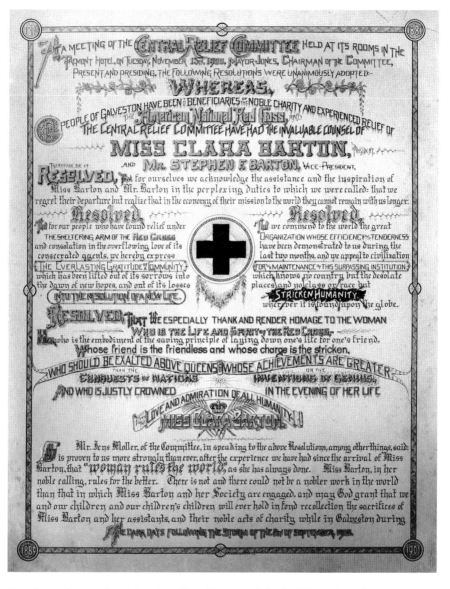

Certificate of appreciation issued to Clara Barton and the Red Cross for their assistance following the 1900 Storm. *Galveston County Museum, Galveston Texas.*

slightest interruption, although from the many and cordial expressions there seems a general reluctance to let her go."

At 4:55 p.m. on November 14, Barton and her committee were taken to the depot in carriages to board the El Sol, a luxury railcar provided as a courtesy of the Pullman Company, and left for Washington.

Barton later wrote, "All this time, the stench of burning flesh penetrated every part of the city. Who could long withstand this?…There was scarcely a well person in Galveston. My helpers grew pale and ill, and even I, who have resisted the effect of so many climes, needed the help of a steadying hand as I walked to the waiting Pullman on the track, courteously tendered to take us away."

# 18

# THE FISHER SISTERS

Many different individuals and partners owned the Tremont House through the years and then leased the proprietorship for others to run the hotel. During one chapter of its operation, it was overseen by an intriguing team of siblings known as the Fisher sisters: Elizabeth "Libby," Nancy Ann, Jane H., Lucy Mariah and their eldest sister, Frances.

Their father, Abel Fisher, set the girls on their lifelong path of running hotels. In 1880, he sold his farm and gristmill to purchase a hotel in Iola, Kansas. Newly widowed, he depended on his daughters to help him run the business. When he passed away, he left his hotel and valuable estate to the young ladies.

With the help of their brother Gilbert, by the early 1890s, the women had expanded their business to include the management of several hotel properties, including the Pierson Hotel in El Paso.

They leased their family hotel in Kansas, moved to Galveston and purchased the well-established Washington Hotel.

In January 1900, the Fishers were sued by employees and the buyer of their Iola hotel. One housekeeper claimed that she had not been paid her $2-a-week wage for 428 weeks but only half of the sum due her. An office clerk also sued for $454 of back salary he claimed was owed. Adding to the lawsuit, the new proprietor sued for payment of items listed in the bill of sale but taken by the sisters, including dishes, bedding, furniture and a long list of items from the hotel.

The sisters acted quickly to settle the $2,000 suit and moved forward to repair their image.

A sample of 1905 Tremont House stationery naming the Fisher sisters as proprietors. *Author's collection.*

Later that year, they would survive the 1900 hurricane in their well-built home at 1818 Church Street, and their hometown newspaper the *Iola Register* happily reported their safety two weeks after the storm.

They sold their interest in the Washington Hotel soon after and leased the Tremont House from its owners in 1902.

Adept at marketing, that year the Fisher sisters hosted an elegant Christmas Day supper at six o'clock for Galveston newspapermen. The guests, however, were not the editors and management of the newspapers but the writers and other blue-collar workers. The evening was complete with music and a lengthy menu, and the special attention made quite an impression on the honorees, who showed their loyalty to their hosts in years to come.

Although their large home was ideal for hosting gatherings, the sisters preferred to focus their attentions on events at the Tremont, and Christmas 1903 was no exception. The rambling menu offered every delicacy available and surely attracted some of Galveston's finest families to enjoy it.

Some of the offerings included were oysters on the half shell, sardine crusts, anchovy canapes, caviar, salted peanuts and almonds, green sea turtle aux quenelles (soup), consommé St. Xavier, broiled lake trout pique, Montpelier butter, chow chow (a pickled relish of summer vegetables), stuffed peppers, pommes Rochambeau, petites bouchees of oysters, sweetbreads,

Montglas lamb cutlets, Maintenon-style timbales of chicken livers à la Talleyrand, apricots à la Richelieu, champagne punch, Kansas City beef demi-glace, new potatoes in cream, French peas, turkey, chestnut dressing, cranberry sauce, cauliflower à la Brisson, spinach en pyramide, roasted leg of venison, currant jelly asparagus tips pompadour, brussels sprouts, lobster salad, graham and cream bread Christmas plum pudding, cognac sauce hot mince pie, orange cream meringue pie, maraschino figs with whipped cream, Charlotte Russe, angel food cake, biscuit glacé, Neapolitan ice cream, assorted fancy cakes, fruits, cheeses and crackers.

That type of extravagance may have caught up the sisters, however, and they soon found themselves back in court.

George Sealy Ewalt and William Gammon, owners of the Tremont House, filed a lawsuit in 1904 against the sisters for failure of payment and lease violations and requested that they vacate the premises.

Tremont Hotel listing in 1905 Galveston directory. *Galveston Texas History Center of the Rosenberg Library, Galveston, Texas.*

Under the terms of the five-year lease, the sisters had agreed to pay the owners 15 percent of the gross profits each month and to keep the hotel in "first-class condition." The owners alleged that those agreements had not been honored.

The sisters filed a countersuit, and laborious details of the proceedings filled the newspapers. An agreement was finally reached between the parties, and all involved decided to divide the duties of maintaining and repairing the hotel. The sisters continued to operate the hotel until the end of their lease in 1907.

Folklore about the sisters that surely sprang from gossip of their day (and perhaps a grain of truth) is what has outlived the women themselves.

According to the tales, after inheriting their father's estate, the unmarried sisters drew up a compact and promised that they would remain together, and in order to better conduct their business, none of them would ever marry. At the time, a legal convention known as coverture put a married woman under her husband's "protection," meaning that women lost many of all of their legal rights to control their own assets. It would be understandable that the Fishers would not want to take that chance.

The *Wichita (KS) Eagle* reported in 1898 that at a point when the sisters were operating three hotels, one sister broke the pact by getting married and was practically disinherited.

One marriage did take place. Elizabeth married James Coates Borwell, a traveling salesman, in Galveston in October 1906, but he deserted her and returned to his home state of Illinois the following February.

The sisters, including Elizabeth, moved to Los Angeles, California, in August 1907.

She sued Borwell for divorce in 1910 on the grounds of desertion. Elizabeth kept the Borwell name but retained her position in the Fisher sisters household.

The remaining four sisters never married.

In January 1912, the sisters sold their home at 1818 Church Street and never returned to the island.

# 19

# THE MISSING MANAGER

On September 4, 1902, the *Galveston Tribune* reported the troubling incident of a missing person. Elmer Dameron Aiken, manager of the Tremont House under the Fisher sisters' proprietorship, was thought to have drowned during a late-night swim in the gulf waters, but his body was nowhere to be found.

Aiken arrived at Murdoch's Bathhouse at about 9:15 p.m. on Wednesday and rented a bathing suit. In that era, it was not common for people to own a swimsuit, so they rented them at bathhouses along the shore.

The twenty-seven-year-old went to dressing room 18, put on a suit and left his clothing and one other item in the room. That item was his false arm, which he had worn since he lost his own arm in an accident several years before. According to custom, he left his keys, money and other valuables in the office of Murdoch's. As he checked the items with the attendant, he commented that he was very hot.

Despite his physical impairment, Aiken was known as an excellent swimmer and was a regular customer at the bathhouse. He was familiar with the water depths in the surrounding area and often swam alone, which was considered unusual.

The water that night was extremely calm, and just before entering it, he encountered John Y. Bedell, a day clerk from the Tremont. Aiken, who appeared to be in a good mood, asked if the water was too warm and Bedell replied that it was fine. Bedell then inquired if the manager had anyone swimming with him, to which he answered that he had come out alone.

Though there were about twenty other bathers in the surf at the time, no one noticed Aiken having any difficulty or leaving.

By 10:00 p.m. all of the bathers who had gone swimming via Murdoch's had returned to gather their belongings, with the exception of Aiken. Mr. Murdoch was anxious to close for the night and sent one of his employees to call "All out," but there was no response to the call.

The employee spotted two people farther down the beach chatting beside a roller bathhouse and assumed that the missing man came across a friend and became distracted. When he approached them, he saw that neither was the man he was searching for, and both individuals confirmed there was no one visible in the water.

Murdoch received this report and immediately started a search by his staff and sent for the police, who joined the search as they arrived. Bathhouse employees treaded the waters in the vicinity while others searched along the shore.

One man took a buggy to a portion of the island where bodies had formerly been discovered on days with similar currents but found nothing. Mounted officers patrolled the beach all night, but no sign of Aiken's body was found.

The items he left behind, including his prosthetic, were turned over to the authorities.

In its report of the tragic situation, the *Tribune* offered several possible explanations, including that Aiken may have swum out too far and become exhausted or that he was overheated and collapsed in the water.

It was mysterious that with so many other bathers in the water no one heard cries for help, but between the noise of people and the surf, his voice might have been drowned out.

Adding to the tragedy was the fact that the young man was engaged to be married in the near future. The couple's original wedding date had been postponed due to the bride's illness, from which she had recovered by that time.

Aiken's father, who lived in Salado, Texas, had recently sent him a check for $264, which was still in the Tremont hotel safe.

As word reached the hotel, his coworkers expressed dismay and sorrow at the loss of the likable man, and the flag atop the hotel was lowered to half-mast.

Headlines the following day brought some degree of relief with the news that Aiken had been located in a hospital in Houston, in a nervous state of collapse.

Aerial view postcard from Tremont House block toward Galveston's beach. *Galveston Texas History Center of the Rosenberg Library, Galveston, Texas.*

A mysterious series of events followed.

Aiken had arrived at the Belmont Hotel in the Fifth Ward of Houston around midnight on the night he disappeared. The night clerk, who didn't notice anything particularly odd about the man other than a haggard appearance, checked Aiken into a room and received payment in advance. He registered under the name Johnson.

The following evening, he telephoned the Houston infirmary and said he needed assistance. A doctor who was a personal friend happened to be in charge of the infirmary that night and, recognizing Aiken, had him admitted at approximately five o'clock.

The doctor noted that although Aiken was neatly dressed, his clothing was stained with mud and he seemed disoriented. Since he had left his previous change of clothes at the bathhouse, it is uncertain where he obtained the ones he later wore.

Aiken told the physician that he must have come to Houston by freight train the night of his disappearance, as the passenger trains did not go to the Fifth Ward. The last thing he remembered was feeling very hot and drinking a lemonade in Galveston—but he could not remember if that was on Wednesday or the day before.

CITY PARK AND BALL HIGH SCHOOL, GALVESTON, TEXAS.

City Park and Ball High School view with Tremont House in the background. *Galveston Texas History Center of the Rosenberg Library, Galveston, Texas.*

It was the doctor's opinion that he was suffering from something akin to nervous prostration caused by his stressful job but ultimately due to delayed effects of a head injury he received during the 1900 Storm.

After he initially received the blow to the head during the hurricane, he forgot his identity for about four months and ended up in California. Along the way, he met another accident and lost his arm while hopping aboard a freight train in El Paso.

Aiken's father was traveling to Galveston from his home in Salado to retrieve the body of his son when he received the telegraph that he was being hospitalized in Houston. After a brief visit with him in the hospital, the father returned home, evidently disgusted at the young man's weakness.

Aiken soon returned to Galveston but never worked in the hotel industry again. He married Galvestonian Margaret Etta Warren on June 11, 1903, but they divorced within five years. There is no record of whether Warren was the young woman to whom he was previously engaged. She remained on the island and never remarried.

Aiken moved east and married Zella Maxey in 1908, and they had one son together. He never saw his Texas family again, telling his new wife that they had a "falling out." The young man who had experienced so much trauma passed away in 1912 at the age of thirty-seven from an unidentified infection. His mental condition was never fully diagnosed.

# 20

# CLOSING THE REGISTER

The Tremont's storm damage from 1900 was repaired, but the years immediately following the hurricane were difficult ones for Galveston. With heroic efforts being focused on rebuilding the city and its infrastructure, the income from tourism was mostly nonexistent for the next decade.

Although still a grand presence and commanding appearance on the skyline, profits from the hotel had difficulty covering the upkeep of such a building. Even so, the Tremont maintained its position as a gathering spot, a location where traveling businessmen could conduct meetings and sales, a full-time residence for some Galvestonians and even a local polling place during elections.

In early April 1928, the owners of Tremont House offered to sell the property to its mortgage holders for $70,000 to get out from under the burden of expenses, but the offer was refused.

The following month, R.J. Kilpatrick, R.M. Fields and J.H. Burnett were elected directors of the Tremont Hotel Company and decided to close the hotel briefly while financial options were considered.

Hotel manager G. McGinley made a trip to New York on June 3 to convince board members to reopen the Tremont on June 15, and several bookings were made at the hotel immediately.

The Tremont remained, at least for the time being, an important place to see and be seen, and visitors to the island who wanted to bring attention to themselves took advantage of that fact. On August 11, visiting daredevil

Erle Seabock announced in the *Daily News* that he would attempt, blindfolded, to climb the corner of the Tremont Hotel without using windows at 6:30 p.m. that day. The previous year, he had driven a car for 135 hours on the beach while chained to the wheel. Authorities were accustomed to stunt performers during the era but objected to the idea of the blindfold and put a stop to the event.

Two weeks later, he attempted to hang beneath an airplane in an innertube on East Beach, but the wind shifted and the plane crashed into the cars along the beach. Luckily, no one—including Seabock, his pilot or bystanders—was hurt. Seabock took his stunts, and questionable judgment, on to the next town.

Whatever the hotel directors' plans were obviously could not save the historic inn from its financial situation, and by fall the hotel's fate was sealed. After several years of owning and operating the landmark, Dr. William Gammon and George Ewalt admitted when questioned that the doors would close permanently on November 1, 1928, six years after celebrating its semicentennial. Employees were given their notice.

The building and its furnishings, though not the land where it stood, had been sold, and preparations had begun for its demolition. According to Dr. Gammon, the property on which the hotel was located would be sold in its entirety or in separate lots.

The announcement was lamented in newspapers throughout Texas and major cities across the United States, but no grand gestures to save the structure were attempted.

Houstonians opened their morning edition of the *Houston Chronicle* on October 28 to the headline "Tremont Hotel—Once the Finest West of New Orleans Doomed to Be Torn Down." Reminiscences were printed with lists of many of the famous and infamous personalities who had stayed within its walls over the years.

October 31 was filled with the last motions of routines that had been occurring for over fifty years: room attendants gathered laundry, bartenders filled glasses, guests packed their bags and descended the grand staircase, breakfast was served, billiard balls clinked, gentlemen visited the barbershop, the lobby newsstand sold papers and transportation to the railroad depot was called for by clerks.

On Halloween night, the last night the famous hostelry would be open, surviving members of the Washington Guard held a reunion in the Tremont Café to bid farewell to the landmark. Seven of them were among the men who had served as a special guard of honor at its opening ceremonies.

Directory listing of Tremont Hotel listing George Ewalt as manager. *Galveston Texas History Center of the Rosenberg Library, Galveston, Texas.*

Former Galvestonian R.D. Bowen, then of Paris, Texas, had suggested the gathering. The special guest of honor was Captain George A. Hill of Houston, the veteran living captain of the organization.

Members signing the roster at the Tremont for the last time included Bowen, Hill, Fred D. Lemcke, Jesse A. Ziegler, Charles Ziegler, Oscar R. Hoecker, Dr. John R. Moore, J. Ed Crain, Sam J. Williams, F. Andler and Fred Erhard.

The men's laughter echoed through the lobby for three hours, recounting daring exploits, parades, victorious competitions and fond memories of friends. It was the last bit of gaiety hosted by the hotel. Once the doors locked at midnight, sentiments were set aside and the process of tearing down the large structure began.

Galveston realtor Hoskins Foster, in charge of much of the property liquidation, ran newspaper advertisements throughout November to announce the sale of all furnishings of the Tremont Hotel, including bedroom suites, carpeting, lobby furniture, light fixtures, an electric light plant and boilers (one of which was "practically new" the ad remarked). The sales were conducted from the hotel storeroom and said to be offered at "giveaway prices."

The contract for razing the building, which began on December 11, was awarded to John Egert, who had established a reputation for his business

Twenty-Third Street view of theaters and Tremont Hotel, circa 1920s. *Courtesy of James Anderson.*

in the aftermath of the 1900 Storm. Permits for the work from the city inspector's office were reported to have cost $9,000.

Salvage from the demolition was sold as the process took place, with the Italian marble, hand-carved woodwork, columns and other extravagant features being of interest to those who could afford them. Uncleaned brick, priced at five dollars per thousand, was acquired by local builders and homeowners as well as businesses from the mainland.

By January 20, 1929, the walls of the Tremont were being demolished down to the third floor in the rear of the building, and work of tearing down the interior had reached the second floor. The slow progress of the project, as well as reports of complaints about the pace of cleaning up the site, were reported for another month before slowly disappearing from the news.

Vestiges, however, remained.

The Tremont Hotel Café, under the management of George Mandich, was relocated to 525 Twenty-First Street within two weeks of the hotel closing. The Tremont Hotel Barber Shop, managed by Joseph DiMare, moved directly across the street from its former place of business.

What appears to be the monogrammed newel post and a portion of the railings and balustrades of the staircase from the ladies' entrance are now part of an unusual architectural creation known as the Santa Fe Castle (or Pignataro Castle) in Santa Fe, Texas. The structure was created from a conglomeration of rescued architectural features from unrelated buildings.

Local architect Michael Gaertner relates that boards from the old Tremont—some with the original paint intact—formed part of an island cottage he lived in several years ago as well.

Tremont walnut tables with marble tops, solid walnut beds with high canopies and even upholstered chairs were purchased by locals as treasured keepsakes of a hotel that had played such an important role in their lives.

Surely there are pieces of furniture, building materials and even plumbing fixtures scattered around Galveston and beyond that have been incorporated into the homes and lives of people who are unaware of their fascinating provenance.

An entire generation would pass before the citizens and visitors of Galveston would be able to walk through the doors of a Tremont House hotel on the island again.

# Part III

—◆—

# A New Beginning

# 21

# BLUM BUILDING

In February 1879, the Leon & J. Blum Company accepted the architectural plans of Eugene T. Heiner for their new establishment located on the northeast corner of Mechanic and Twenty-Fourth Streets. Tax records for the lots show that the land was vacant, mostly likely due to any previous structures being lost in the large conflagration in the business district in 1877. The Blums had lost their previous establishment on the corner of the Strand and Twenty-Second Street in the same tragedy.

The design was for a flat-roofed, 120-foot-square, three-story structure. Constructed entirely of red brick, it would be stuccoed to resemble stone and feature ornamental facings, cornice and trim.

Before construction began, the lot was filled with soil taken from ships in port. Many at that time used soil as ballast, which would be emptied on arrival to make room for their cargo. The ships, which came from around the world, therefore provided a foundation for the building that had international connections of a unique sort.

Its first floor was designed with a continuous series of bays with double doors; the second and third were pierced with large Romanesque-style windows. These, in addition to ceilings that soared sixteen feet, six inches in height, helped to flood the interiors with light and provided superior ventilation.

Construction was completed in 1880, but by 1881 the growing business required more space. The Blums purchased adjoining lots on the same block to allow for expansion.

Illustration of Leon & H. Blum Company. *Courtesy of Michael Gaertner.*

Heiner's work was expanded by architect Nicholas Clayton, and an east end addition was completed in June 1882. Further additions and improvements were contracted to Clayton in 1883 and 1884, increasing the frontage on Mechanic to a remarkable 250 feet in length.

By the time the new iteration of the building was completed for the 1885 city directory, Clayton had added cornice details and a sloping mansard roof (though a cityscape artist depicted it with a truncated hip roof the same year) punctuated with dormer windows and topped with metal cresting.

Clayton worked on the building once more in November 1887 to provide a "new office addition" to the interior.

With a footprint of over 100,000 feet, the Blums had ample space to display the largest selection of goods in the South. The vast spaces with wood floors and ceilings were designed with no intervening walls, allowing aisles to be set up contiguously from wall to wall. Wood columns forty inches in diameter were placed fifteen feet apart throughout to support the weight of the structure.

The front and center of the first floor were set aside for the office and accounting department of the company, attractively finished in varnished cypress. Important papers were kept in the latest model safes manufactured by Diebold safe, which listed the Blums in advertisements as respected customers.

Directly behind this was the essential shipping department, organized in one of the new building additions. Each department was assigned its own shipping clerk, and as goods were sent to the department for delivery, the individual clerks would double-check each item for accuracy.

The shipping department was especially important because of the high percentage of orders received via mail or telegraph from customers across the United States and Mexico and in Indian Territory, some resulting from the work of traveling salesmen.

Each department also had a buyer who traveled abroad for about nine months each year in the manufacturing centers of Europe and the United States.

Because much of the merchandise displayed was samples, once an item was selected and purchased, the order would be sent to the check clerks who officed next to shipping. After examining the customer orders, they would dispatch another employee to fetch the appropriate items from the firm's warehouse on Avenue A and Twenty-Second Street. After retrieving the order, the clerks would then double-check the items before they were delivered to the customers.

It was said that between the main building and its warehouse, Blums frequently had enough merchandise in-house or in transit to fill another identical store.

Beside the check room was an impressively compact hoist engine room housing the equipment that enabled the hydraulic freight elevators to lift twelve thousand pounds at a time.

The transport of goods to and from the docks and depots was a daily affair, and an open space in front of the engine room operated as a loading dock that could admit a dozen drays at once. Twenty-five drays—horse or mule-drawn wagons without sides—were employed at all times.

Due to the southern scarcity of light wood like white pine, the room next to the loading dock was organized as a box room, where carpenters were employed to build completed boxes from skeleton frames sent from the East Coast.

On the west end of the ground floor at the back of the store, customers found the ladies' and children's clothing and linen departments.

Silks, velvets, ginghams and satins crowded the ladies' area. Here, women could purchase premade clothing or yardage for themselves or their children. Seamstresses found cloth ranging in price from seventy-five cents to fifty dollars per yard in every color and fabric imaginable. Ready-made dresses, skirts, shawls, blouses and private garments for every occasion could also be purchased.

Blum's clerks were never allowed to say, "We haven't got it," as anything not in their current stock could be ordered.

The pride of the linen area was the fine California white merino blankets, of which the Blums led national sales. They also offered a variety of other blankets and flannels to warm both thrifty and well-to-do customers in the chilly months.

The area dedicated to menswear may have been far less colorful than the ladies', but it offered quality clothing for every taste from "a sailor, a farmer, a mechanic, or a gentleman of leisure."

Guests could ascend one of two deep-stepped, wide stairways to the second floor or opt to sit in a chair aboard the elevator to ride to their next destination.

The second floor of the establishment was entirely dedicated to notions, which were fancy goods such as stationery, cutlery, musical instruments, thread, jewelry, hosiery, laces, embroidery, gloves, Swiss ribbons, needles, pins and threads, small housewares, combs and buttons and laces from Saxony.

This area was considered the "women's matter," as men feigned to have no interest in browsing through such minor items. Their furnishings were gathered in a single area to the side, but not intermingled with, the above-mentioned goods.

A profusion of masculine valises, trunks, canes, duffle bags, umbrellas, buckskin gloves, dress shirts, suspenders, ties, monocles, suits, work jeans, overalls, raincoats and undergarments was available to gentlemen shoppers on the second floor.

Customers could once again use the elevator or one of the two stairways to reach the third floor, which housed the shoe and hat departments.

The Blum's boot and shoe section for ladies, children, and gentlemen offered the largest in-house selection of footwear in the nation, with an astounding twelve thousand cases of footgear kept in stock. It was the only department that exclusively carried American-made goods. Everything from ladies' dancing slippers to men's leather work boots could be found there.

Once finished shopping for shoes, customers could browse the hat and cap section for the entire family as well. American to French, functional to fancy, styles from twenty-five cents to fifty-five dollars apiece were available.

Not surprisingly, the firm sold approximately $5 million worth of merchandise each year.

# 22

# ARCHITECT EUGENE T. HEINER

Eugene Thomas Heiner was the architect responsible for the Leon & H. Blum Building on Mechanic Street, home to the current Tremont House.

Born in New York to German immigrant parents, Heiner apprenticed to the prominent architect J.A. Vrydaugh in Terre Haute, Indiana. Working as a draftsman, he learned the intricacies of design from his Belgian supervisor, who was known for his designs of public buildings and courthouses throughout the United States and Europe.

Heiner completed his training in Germany.

While still a teenager, he entered a design competition at the Philadelphia Centennial Exposition in 1876 against forty-two competitors and won first prize. He used the prize money from the competition to move to Texas, and there he met and married Viola Isenhour in 1878.

The couple moved to Houston, where he practiced architecture for the rest of his life. They were the parents of four girls: Mabel, Viola, Jennie and Hazel.

That same year, Heiner received his first major commission, for the Galveston County jail at Twentieth and Winnie Streets.

On February 19, 1879, Heiner's proposed plans for the new Blum building at the corner of Mechanic and Twenty-Fourth Streets were adopted. An impressive 120 feet square, it would be composed of cemented brickwork and surmounted by an iron cornice. Once constructed, it became a commanding presence in Galveston's downtown.

His major commercial work included Galveston's Kauffman and Runge Building (1882) and several structures in Houston, including the Brashear Building (1882), Houston Cotton Exchange and Board of Trade Building (1884), W.L. Foley Building (1889, now on the National Register), Sweeney and Coombs Opera House (1890) and Houston Ice and Brewing Company plant (1893).

Four angels incorporated into the Modern Renaissance design of the Cotton Exchange design are believed to represent his four daughters.

Heiner's work is still revered for its beauty and functionality. Through the years, the talented creator incorporated intricate accents into his designs and featured work in a variety of styles, such as Italianate, Romanesque Revival, High Victorian, Richardson Romanesque and Second Empire. Whenever possible, though, his favored High Victorian detailing also made an appearance.

Somewhat appropriately, Heiner's offices in his building on Main Street in Houston were recognized as one of the most elegantly furnished and finished of any office in the South.

When structural problems were encountered in the erection of the state capitol building in Austin in 1887, expert architects Nicholas Clayton of Galveston, Heiner of Houston and B.A. Harrod of New Orleans were summoned to address the stability and safety of the project. Their amended plans involved strengthening the dome with a series of steel beams, steel uprights and braces and correcting the inadequate thickness of work on the dome. They were hailed for saving the project.

In addition to residential work for wealthy clients, Heiner gained renown for his courthouses and jails in twenty-nine counties throughout Texas. After his success designing a jail for Galveston County, jail commissions followed for other counties such as Bastrop, Coleman, Colorado, Gonzales, Harris, Montgomery, Smith, Tarrant, Victoria and Wharton. His courthouse plans were used in the counties of Austin, Brazos, Dewitt, Falls, Harris, Jasper, Jefferson, Lavaca, Matagorda, Montgomery, Polk and Trinity.

His institutional architecture included several buildings at the Agricultural and Mechanical College of Texas (now Texas A&M University), multiple public schools and the State Penitentiary in Huntsville.

Heiner passed away in Houston on April 26, 1901, at the age of forty-eight after a long illness. Many friends and admirers attended the funeral at his home at Milam and Hadley Streets and reminisced about the talented man's genial nature. He was buried in Washington Cemetery in Houston, joining his wife, who died twelve years earlier. Though only forty-eight when he died, the founding member of the Texas Association of Architects left a legacy of beautiful buildings, many of which are still admired to this day.

23

# THE MERCHANT PRINCE

L eon Blum was known as the Merchant Prince of Texas. It was a title well-earned after years as a tradesperson alongside his brothers and other partners. Known for his honesty and progressive business tactics, he was admired by his friends and associates.

Born in Alsace in 1836, he apprenticed as a tinsmith but decided to follow in his father's footsteps as a salesman instead. At only fifteen years of age, he moved to America to join his older brother Alexander in Louisiana in February 1852.

He worked as a traveling salesman for his brother's company for about eighteen months before moving to Richmond, Texas, where his sibling had established A. Blum & Co.

In 1859, the pair then moved their business to Galveston, which was a large commerce and financial center in the state. They joined as partners and established a house of trade in a frame building on the southeast corner of Avenue D and Tremont Street. Their business had already

Portrait of Leon Blum (1837–1906).
*Galveston Texas History Center of the Rosenberg Library, Galveston, Texas.*

become successful by the time Texas seceded from the Union and joined the Confederacy during the Civil War.

Leon married Henrietta Levy in 1862, and they had two daughters together. The prominent merchant family moved to Houston to avoid the wartime hostilities. Over the next few years, they moved to Brownsville and Matamoros, Mexico, where they adjusted their stock to suit the needs of the time and flourished under the name H. Blum & Co.

After the war ended, the Blums returned to Galveston in the fall of 1865 to reestablish their business. There Leon utilized the different purchasing strategies he learned during the lean war years to increase his ventures, eventually expanding his dry import and cotton business to be the largest in Texas.

The new firm of Leon & H. Blum, comprising brothers Leon, Alexander and Sylvain Blum and cousins Hyman and Joseph Blum, was founded late in 1868 and became the city's leading importer and dealer in wholesale goods for the next two decades. Their business encompassed states in the Southwest, Indian Territory and Mexico and operated from offices in Galveston, New York, Boston and Paris, France.

The flourishing partnership did over $1 million in business in 1870 and opened a spacious four-story building at Twenty-Second Street and the Strand in June of the same year.

Tragedy arrived for the Blum family that October, however, when Joseph Blum, Henry Blum and Charles Blum were killed during the sinking of the steamship *Varuna*. They were returning from a trip to New York when the ship was struck by a storm off Florida. Out of the entire crew and thirty-six passengers, mostly from Texas, all but five crew members perished.

Six years later, Leon suffered a further loss when his wife, Henrietta, passed away at age of thirty-five.

Perhaps because he had weathered so much tragedy earlier in the decade, when it visited again in 1877, Leon bore it with a remarkable presence of mind. That year, a fire began on Market Street and swept across Mechanic Street and the Strand, leaving twenty-six buildings in the business district, including the Blum's store, in ruins.

Within days, Leon reordered stock and rented a number of local storefronts, such as the newly constructed Bolton Building, and was doing business again.

Leon & H. Blum erected a grand new flagship building on Mechanic Street in 1880 that became known as the Blum Building. This structure still stands today and is home to the current Tremont House hotel.

Leon & H. Blum Building in the 1930s. *Historic American Buildings Survey Collection, Courtesy Library of Congress Prints and Photographs Division, Washington, D. C.*

Blum's firm was one of the stockholders of the Gulf, Colorado and Santa Fe Railway, and he worked to improve rail links to the interior of the state. A small town was founded on the line in Hill County in 1881 and named Blum in his honor.

Expanding his business interests, the Leon & H. Blum Land Company was incorporated in 1882 and opened offices at Twenty-Fourth and Mechanic. Leon Blum was the firm's president, his brother Sylvain Blum was its vice president and A. Ferrier was its secretary and treasurer.

The land company was the largest land and livestock company based in Galveston in that era and had tracts of land for sale in 150 Texas counties ranging in size from 1 to 156,000 acres.

After they constructed and opened the Blum Building, it became one of the leading wholesale houses in the South and employed two hundred people.

Blum was active in the community as well as his own endeavors. He was instrumental in the erection of the second Tremont House and the Cotton Exchange Building, served as president of the Wharves Company and represented Galveston in Washington, D.C., during the discussions of the Deep Water Project. He also contributed to the Bayland Orphan's Home for Boys and a number of schools.

After an impressive life, Leon Blum passed away at his home in Galveston on April 28, 1906, at the age of sixty-nine and was buried in the Hebrew Cemetery.

## 24

# MISTROTS AND NEWSPAPERMEN

To the surprise of the entire community, the Blum importing and dry goods business was declared insolvent on March 25, 1896. There had been no indication of trouble before the announcement. The following day, the *News* declared that "the knowledge came like a thunderbolt out of a clear sky…and was the subject of discussion upon the streets during the greater part of the day."

The company had endured the 1873 depression, but the poor economy in the 1890s was more than it could ride out. Plans were considered to reorganize the firm, but it did not happen. The Leon & H. Blum Land Company, which was operated separately, survived.

Two weeks later, Mistrot Bros. & Co. had purchased the complete stock of Leon & H. Blum, signed a three-year lease on the building and made plans to transport its Houston warehouse holdings to the island by June 1. In order to reduce the amount of stock, the company announced that there would be a sale with greatly reduced prices

On June 6, a newspaper article reported that the lower floor of the building was "in the hands of carpenters" who were preparing to transform it into an immense wholesale and retail establishment that would offer "six stores under one roof."

An impressive 780 feet of shelving was installed with another 200 feet to be added for a millinery department that would be in an area previously used as an office.

Interior view of Mistrot & Bros. store in the Blum Building. *Galveston Texas History Center of the Rosenberg Library, Galveston, Texas.*

The majority of the upper two floors were used for the wholesale business, but the lower floor, with the exception of the packing and shipping room on the east end, would be converted into what the Mistrots advertised as the "most complete department store in the South."

Arranged from east to west on the ground floor, aisles offered dry goods, house furnishings, notions, clothing and furnishing goods for gentlemen, boots, shoes and millinery. A ladies' department, complete with perfumery, would occupy a section of the second floor.

The grand opening sale of "Blum bankrupt stock" began on June 28 and promised to sell $230,000 worth of goods at less than the cost of their production. The extensive inventory took longer to disperse than initially planned, and the sale finally ended the first week of September.

The business was a success, and many tourists to the island prioritized a visit to the store. The Mistrot name was well known throughout the state, having fifty-one stores in addition to the Galveston location.

The hurricane of 1900 sent surge waters up to the second floor of the wholesale house. Family members and clerks worked diligently to move the majority of the stock upstairs to safety.

The Mistrot brothers, who by this time had partnered with Louis A. Adoue, purchased the building in 1913, and from 1914 to 1917 the company was known as Mistrot & Adoue.

The company moved their interests off the island in 1917, and from 1919 to 1923 the building on Mechanic Street was vacant.

The Adoue family sold the building and lots to the *Galveston Tribune*, a weekday afternoon newspaper, in 1923.

The paper made several changes to the interior of the building to accommodate the press, but none to the exterior. An open house event was held to show off the *Tribune*'s new home on June 27, 1924, but two years later the building would be empty again.

Purchased by the News Publishing Company, which also owned the *Galveston Daily News* at 2108 Mechanic Street, the Tribune's staff was consolidated in December 1926 and their press equipment and furnishings sold off to the public.

Before the structure was fully emptied of its contents, advertisements began to appear listing the building for lease as warehouse space.

Stationer F.E. Erhart leased part of the building in 1927 and was joined the following year by the offices of the Galveston Builders Exchange. In 1930, they were joined by the second newspaper to occupy the building, the *Galveston Commercial Reporter*, which was in business from 1928 to 1938.

In 1941, the Electric Supply Company operated out of the building, and part of the east end of the ground floor became the New Garage parking structure.

News Publishing Company sold the building to Jimmy Lee Graber in 1963, who in turn sold it to Arthur L. Peck and his wife, Delores, in 1973.

The Home Furniture Company operated on the first floor of the west end in the 1970s.

Dolores A. Peck's estate sold the massive building to the Galveston Historical Foundation in 1980.

# 25

# McDONNELL BUILDING

The four-story Frank McDonnell Building is located on the northwest corner of Tremont and Mechanic Streets. With each different owner over the years, the name of the hotel in this structure has changed. Even the land it sits on has a legacy of hospitality that stretches back to the earliest days of Galveston and has been home to the San Jacinto House, Palmetto House, Royal Hotel, Stirling Hotel, New Tremont Hotel, Milner Hotel and the Belmont Hotel—all before becoming a part of the current Tremont House.

## SAN JACINTO HOUSE

French immigrant Alphonse Aulanier purchased the property from John D. Grosbeck in 1839 and built the San Jacinto House hotel and restaurant there in 1841. A portion of a building formerly used as a courthouse was moved from Avenue G to the property to incorporate into the wood-frame hotel.

He became well known for his French cooking and cordiality at the restaurant. Having begun his business when Texas was a republic, he was a citizen of the new state of Texas within a few years.

Galveston was home to a large and tight-knit community of former French citizens, and on April 23, 1848, there was a banquet held at the Alphonse Hotel to give them an opportunity to honor and memorialize the Parisians lost in the French Revolution, which had occurred two months earlier.

Unfortunately, the host of the event died as he was planning the event, and on the same date as the banquet Aulanier's probate notice was in the news.

What Monsieur Aulanier is remembered for, though, is not his cooking but for a decision he made before his death. In his will, he specified manumission of his slave Julie, providing her freedom and an inheritance of $300 "without the right of any person to contest the same in any manner." It was the first act of manumission of an enslaved person recorded in Galveston County.

# PALMETTO HOUSE

Aulanier's heirs, who by 1850 had changed the name of the hotel from San Jacinto House to Palmetto Hotel, leased the proprietorship of the inn.

The 1850 census lists Palmetto innkeepers as thirty-three-year-old E. Blakeman, who lived there with his wife and three daughters, and thirty-year-old Charles Fowler. They advertised the hotel as employing a porter who "was always ready on the arrival of boats to convey baggage to the hotel."

The following year, the establishment served as a voting precinct under Blakeman and Fowler's supervision.

They offered boarding, or meals, as well as rooms and advertised that they were able to accommodate "thirty to forty day boarders at fair prices." Breakfast was served at 7:00 a.m., dinner (the midday meal) at 1:00 p.m. and supper at 7 p.m.

Irish immigrant Bernard J. McDonnell, who previously worked as the innkeeper of Galveston's Columbia Hotel, purchased the Palmetto House in 1854 and moved in with his wife, Winifred and their four children. Three years later he completely renovated and refurnished the hotel to put forward a more fashionable image.

It was not uncommon for "permanent guests" to run their own businesses from hotels in that era, and that included doctors as well as salesmen. Patients of Dr. D'Alton, who claimed to have once served the British royal household, could access his "office" via a private entrance at the furthest door of the Palmetto on Mechanic Street.

The *News* made a reference to McDonnell's "weighty spouse" Winifred in July 1865, stating that the woman, who was called "Madame Mac" in the community, was known for her benevolence and hospitality.

For over a decade, including the Civil War years, a native of Paris, France, named Jean Baptiste Bavoux operated a barbershop on the first floor of the Palmetto House.

A passerby one night in November 1866 helped avert disaster when he noticed that someone had stacked wooden crates against the back of the hotel and set them on fire. Fortunately, he made the discovery before any damage was done. The culprit was never caught, but the motive was thought to be a disgruntled customer or competitor.

McDonnell and his son Frank closed the hotel briefly from mid-August to September in 1868 to make repairs before Frank became the hotel's official proprietor.

In July 1869, Galveston businessmen sponsored a trip to the island for residents of the Bayland Orphan's Home for Boys, an institution near Morgan's Point that was founded to care for orphans of Confederate veterans. During their stay, Palmetto House volunteered to entertain and provide accommodations for twenty-five of the youngsters.

A second attempt at arson occurred in September 1869, when wooden barrels beside the building were set on fire. Once again, the deed was spotted before much damage was done, and the hook and ladder company was able to extinguish the flames.

The foreshadowing of destruction by fire finally came to pass when the hotel burned to the ground in the Moro Castle fire of December 3, 1869, which destroyed several blocks of the downtown district.

At a city meeting regarding the aftermath of the devastating fire, McDonnell proposed the idea of constructing a new hotel on the land where the Palmetto had stood, but it was met with indifference.

## McDonnell Building

In 1870, Bernard formally deeded the empty lots to his son Francis "Frank" McDonnell, who replaced the lost hotel with a three-story brick commercial structure.

Facing Tremont Street with a corner entrance at Tremont and Mechanic Streets, the rectangular structure featured a cast-iron ground floor façade with large, hooded arch windows. The lobby was ornamented with multicolored patterned tile flooring, a pressed tin ceiling and an elegant wood staircase that rose to an atrium and opened onto the second and third floors. The upper floors had pine floors and pressed tin walls. The cistern was located on the roof.

Its proximity to the wharves, railroad lines, banks and businesses on the Strand made it an ideal location for office and store space.

One of the well-known tenants was Denis Neil, a tailor who moved into the building in September 1871. There he established an elegant store that offered hats, furnishing goods and clothing. Neil also, of course, carried a variety of cloth and patterns, from which his employee E.R. Stewart could direct the tailoring of custom clothing.

Other lessees over the next two decades included a hardware store, harness shop, trunk store, wholesale grocery and bank.

Frank died at the young age of thirty-three in 1876, leaving a wife and two children. As executor of his son's will, Bernard sold the property to T.C. Thompson for Elizabeth Stevens in 1880. She in turn sold it to Reverend Jesse M. Callaway, a purchasing clerk just branching out into real estate dealings. During the years he owned the structure, he and his family lived in various boardinghouses and hotels, including the Tremont House.

The structure changed hands again in 1902 when Callaway defaulted on payment of a loan made in 1897 by widow Isabella Dyer Kopperl.

Two months after her death in May 1902 the executors of her estate foreclosed on the hotel property and sold it to the highest bidder at auction. The highest bidders, who paid $13,000, were B.J. Kopperl, Herman Benjamin Kopperl, Moritz Kopperl and Joseph Osterman Dyer—family members and executors of the estate.

# ROYAL HOTEL

With Herman Kopperl as its new proprietor, a fourth story was added to the structure in 1906 by Galveston architect Donald N. McKenzie, and the building was renamed the Hotel Royal.

Guest rooms had paneled wood doors with transoms for ventilation, and each room had its own sink with running water. A stairway to the fourth floor was added at the rear of the building.

The Hotel Royal Bar, with a corner entrance and frontage on Mechanic Street, was operated by Gustave B. Franck. The tile threshold with the wording "Royal Bar" that still exists at the entrance at the corner of Twenty-Third and Mechanic Streets dates from that time.

The Hotel Royal Café was operated by Frank W. Schmitz, who would soon become manager of the hotel.

Three more stories were added to the Hotel Royal in 1909 by Houston architect Henry C. Cooke and contractor C.C. Wenzel. It was such an impressive project for the time that Wenzel used an illustration of the seven-story hotel in his future ads.

At this time, the proprietors added a brass cage elevator that traveled to the sixth floor, where guests could then transfer to stairs to the seventh floor.

Herman passed away in 1915 and left the bulk of his estate, including the hotel, to his wife, Sara Ann "Nana" Kopperl. Seven years later, she married John Joseph Stirling, who became the manager of the hotel in 1924.

Nana was sent to Fredericksburg for her health, under a doctor's orders, and she passed away there on June 29, 1927, at the age of fifty-five. During the lengthy litigation of her estate, Stirling acted as the manager of the hotel.

The year following his wife's death, he was faced with a calamity at the Royal.

At about 11:40 p.m. on February 23, 1928, employees were alerted of a fire on the seventh floor.

Just as bellboy Sandy Thompson reached the front desk to see night clerk Theodore L. Brusig telephone the Central Fire Station, the elevator crashed to the ground floor from above. Brusig sent attendants to wake guests and bring them from their rooms. Many attempted to ring for the now inoperable elevator before being ushered down the stairwells. Thirty-six guests escaped without injury.

The fire spread rapidly, assisted by a strong north wind, and sparks began to fly from the windows. Fire Chief R. H. Westerlage, who saw the embers might endanger surrounding structures, immediately sounded a general alarm.

The biggest obstacle in fighting the flames was the height of the seven-story building. The fire spread under the roof eaves and burst through the windows of the top floor.

Firemen from the first two units to respond to the scene reported that there was no pressure on the hotel standpipe, so hose lines provided on each floor of the hotel were of no use. Each had to be connected to a pumper in order to produce a strong enough stream to reach the fire at the top of the one-hundred-foot hotel, and at one point eleven streams were being produced from five pumper wagons.

Royal Hotel, Galveston, Texas.

*Above*: Royal Bar tile threshold outside former entrance of the Belmont Hotel, now the Tremont House. *Photo by author.*

*Opposite*: Postcard of seven-story Royal Hotel. *Author's collection.*

The men pulled the heavy hose up stairwells to reach the seventh-floor machinery of the elevator, where the fire originated, and two lines were taken in through a window from the south fire escape.

Other lines were positioned atop the Washington Hotel and the two-story building north of the Royal.

As a result of the massive effort, the majority of the fire was contained to the seventh floor, although flames were sucked down a chimney and caused an outbreak on the northwest corner of the fifth floor.

The roof collapsed inward on the seventh floor and part of the sixth, but due to the fact that the stories added in 1909 were constructed of reinforced concrete, no further walls collapsed.

After two and a half hours of battling the blaze, it was brought under control shortly before 2:00 a.m. Damage to the lower floors was mainly due to water, which seeped through the floors and ceilings.

Between one and three o'clock in the morning, one or more looters ransacked several rooms, including Stirling's apartment on the third floor, where they absconded with a diamond stick pin, an automatic pistol, a signet ring, a watch chain and a cuff link set. Other rooms on the fourth floor were also vandalized, but not to the same degree.

Stirling reported to the newspaper that damage was estimated at $32,000 and his insurance covered $15,000, but he promised to reopen by May 1 of that year complete with improvements throughout the hotel.

Stirling, who assumed all costs in the repair and renovation of the Royal, sued Moritz, Isadore and Herman Kopperl on April 22, 1928, for full possession of the hotel and its improvements and won.

The heavily damaged seventh floor had to be removed, and the Royal was converted into a six-story building with office and shop space on the first floor, with a coffee shop taking the place of the bar.

## Stirling Hotel / New Tremont

The hotel became the Stirling Hotel, but once the grand Tremont House was torn down, Stirling renamed his house the New Tremont. The hotel was alternately known by both names.

Revitalized and refurnished, the ninety-room hotel reopened on June 27, 1928, with an enlarged lobby, the addition of plate-glass windows to improve lighting and updated ventilation.

Stirling took a second wife just days before the grand reopening when he married twenty-eight-year-old Ruth K. Vautrin, a teacher at Ball High School. After their wedding, she retired from teaching and took over management of the coffee shop.

That fall, the owners marketed special winter rates for "permanents" and "transients" of $1.00 to $1.50 per day, and rooms with baths for $1.50 and $2.00.

Stirling leased out the management of the hotel by October 1929 to Louie Jack and Augusta Adams, who owned the Oriental Hotel on Avenue F at Twenty-First Street. Part of the renovations that took place under his supervision was the installation of telephones throughout the building.

The following month, the hotel witnessed excitement as the "Little Aggies" football team overnighted there before a hotly contested grudge match football game with the Ball High Tornadoes. Happily for locals, the undefeated Ball defeated the visiting team 29–0.

A newspaper advertisement printed Thanksgiving week of 1929 announced low seasonal rates for the New Tremont Hotel, explaining that it was formerly known as the Stirling. It listed amenities as one hundred modern rooms, an elevator and hot and cold showers. Single rooms without a bath were five dollars per day, and those with a bath were eight dollars.

Two fires broke out in one day on July 18, 1932, at the New Tremont. The first, believed to have been caused by electrical equipment in the elevator, occurred at 5:25 a.m. By the time firefighters arrived, the penthouse apartment was in flames, but they managed to extinguish them before extensive damage was done.

After eight o'clock that morning, while the marshal was inspecting the scene to determine the exact cause of the ignition, he discovered another fire between the walls of the fourth floor on the northwest side of the hotel. He immediately summoned the fire department, which succeeded in squelching the difficult-to-access flames by threading hoses through fourth- and sixth-story windows.

This time, damage was contained to a handful of rooms, and the hotel was able to remain open.

Financial strain during the Depression meant that not many families could afford elaborate holiday decorations, so newspapers listed local businesses that displayed festive arrangements that could be visited. Stirling's New Tremont was included in that list in December 1937 as having a fully festooned Christmas tree.

# MILNER HOTEL / BELMONT HOTEL

Hotel owner Stirling and his wife divorced in 1942, and she returned to the teaching profession. Part of the divorce settlement required Stirling to pay his ex-wife $15,000 for her interest in the Stirling Hotel building, with the exception of the coffee shop.

When the divorce was finalized, he leased the property to Milner Hotels, Incorporated, a hotel chain that planned to capitalize on America's new fascination with car travel on the ever-expanding highway system. They renamed it the Milner Hotel.

Though the Milner group attempted to purchase the hotel, Stirling sold it to Pearl and Isadore Meyer Geller in 1945 for $41,000.

Through the 1950s, the Gellers retained the hotel in much the same state as they purchased it and charged five to six dollars per week for a room. The residents often ran advertisements in the newspaper when they had something to sell, were looking for someone or were offering work. In 1947, one such ad was put forth by Mr. Shire and Mr. Shinkle, who lived in room 507 and wanted to sell their 1940 Pontiac Coupe.

The owners often purchased space in the *News* to extend greetings to their community for various holidays.

Being a public establishment for so many years guaranteed a high likelihood of colorful characters occasionally making an appearance and one time resulted in a monkey on the loose. P.A. Smith, a resident of the hotel in 1954, had kept the small white-faced monkey as a pet for three years. One Saturday night, Smith left the creature in his car when he stopped at a diner near Sixth Street and Seawall to eat and was surprised when the monkey was no longer there when he returned. The owner claimed to have left it before without incident.

Another incident occurred in July 1957 when Ernest Carroll Mitchell of Borger, Texas, ran amuck in the hotel and adjoining café, causing an estimated $2,300 in damage. He claimed that "Indians" were chasing him with machine guns but could not remember what tribe. He was arrested on eight different charges but released until his hearing, for which he did not appear.

The hotel changed names one more time when the Gellers redubbed it the Hotel Belmont, which was usually referred to as the Belmont Hotel, around 1961.

In the 1960s, it operated largely as a residence hotel, and many of its tenants were seamen. Rates were eight dollars and up per week, and the amenity of a television set was added to the lobby.

A 1980s view of the four-story Belmont Hotel, showing garage entrance to Blum Building on the left. *Courtesy of The Tremont House.*

Rex Galloway, a resident of Clear Lake, was leaving the nearby Kon Tiki Club at about midnight one Sunday in November 1979 when he smelled smoke. The twenty-eight-year-old knocked on the door of the hotel and asked the clerk if they had an incinerator and was told no.

At about the same time, a smoke detector went off on the sixth floor, and while the clerk called the fire department, Galloway ran to the top floor to begin alerting residents. The young man and others rallied to wake anyone else in the smoke-filled structure, and once everyone was on their way to safety, he attempted to use the fire hoses on the fourth and fifth floors, but they were inoperable.

Eight units of the fire department arrived and fought the fire, which had broken out between the ceiling of the sixth floor and the roof, and contained it within three hours. Damage was contained to the burned ceiling, and no one was injured.

The Geller family continued to own and operate the Belmont until it was sold to George P. Mitchell for redevelopment in May 1981.

# 26

# GEORGE AND CYNTHIA WOODS MITCHELL

George Phydias Mitchell was born on May 21, 1919, in Galveston to Greek immigrant parents of modest means who operated a cleaning business.

In order to fund his studies at Texas A&M University, he waited tables in residence halls, sold candy, built bookcases and had a tailoring concession. In 1940, he graduated first in his class in petroleum engineering and took a job with Amoco working in the East Texas and Louisiana oil fields.

When World War II began, Mitchell joined the Army Corps of Engineers and was stationed in his hometown of Galveston, where he oversaw corps projects. He soon reached the rank of lieutenant.

Cynthia Loretta Woods was born in New York City in 1922 but moved to Illinois as a child with her twin sister and was raised by a single mother during the Depression. After the girls finished high school, the family moved to Houston, and the young ladies studied fine arts at the University of Houston while helping to support their mother.

Cynthia and George met on a Thanksgiving Day train ride after attending a Texas A&M versus University of Texas football game with friends.

They married in a double wedding ceremony alongside Cynthia's sister Pamela in 1943.

During the war years, while George was in the corps, Cynthia worked as a secretary for a military officer. After the war, the couple, who eventually had ten children, moved to Houston.

Mitchell worked as a consulting geologist and later began a wildcatting operation with his brother and another partner. He later formed Mitchell Energy and Development.

George Mitchell, who is considered the father of hydraulic fracturing, participated in operating approximately ten thousand wells during his career, including more than one thousand wildcats.

As their fortune grew, George and Cynthia Mitchell conscientiously gave back to their communities. An example of this is the fact that George made donations topping $95 million to Texas A&M University, becoming the largest benefactor in history to the same school where he had worked multiple jobs to pay for his own tuition and housing.

The Mitchells considered Galveston Island their second home in the 1970s and 1980s and looked for ways they could contribute to the town's precarious economic situation. They were distressed by the loss of so many historic buildings on the island, including several Broadway mansions, the Ursuline Convent and the Quarantine Station. The couple shared a vision of the restoration of historic architecture and how it would likely rejuvenate the local economy.

During a trip to Savannah, Georgia, in 1972, Mitchell became aware of an innovative preservation program there that operated by purchasing and reselling historic properties with a revolving fund. Encouraged by the promise of the method, he sent members of the Galveston Historical Foundation to study it and reimplement it locally.

Mitchell was aware, however, that such funds would not be sufficient to save the number of significant buildings in danger of being lost. He and Cynthia dedicated themselves to revitalizing the architectural history of Galveston, beginning with the purchase of the 1871 League Building in 1976, which they restored in 1979.

Cynthia was chosen by the National Trust for Historic Preservation to serve on its board. She and George endowed the Cynthia Woods Mitchell Fund for Historic Interiors within that organization, where she played a pivotal role as a member of the grants selection committee.

Her eye for design and impeccable taste was a key advantage in the couple's restoration work.

In the Strand District alone, they were responsible for the restoration of seventeen commercial buildings, as well as other areas of the island. Among their projects were the Marine-Heidenheimer Building, the old Washington Hotel, the Rosenberg Building, the John Berlocher Building, the Hotel Galvez (currently known as the Grand Galvez), the Pier 21

Cynthia Woods Mitchell (1922–2009) and George Phydias Mitchell (1919–2013) in front of Tremont House. *Galveston Texas History Center of the Rosenberg Library, Galveston, Texas.*

complex on the harbor and the Harbor House and Marina, using millions of dollars of their own.

With a goal of providing a first-class hotel to service the Historic Strand District, the Mitchells purchased the 1879 Leon and H. Blum Building and Belmont Hotel on Mechanic Street between Twenty-Third and Twenty-Fourth Streets.

The renovation that would become the Tremont Hotel was one of ten restoration projects that they worked on concurrently in downtown Galveston, using an estimated $25 million of private funds.

The showpiece hotel opened its doors in 1985, and the Mitchells revived Galveston's long-dormant Mardi Gras as part of the celebration.

Cynthia's favorite room at the Tremont House was in the Belmont wing, where she spent many happy hours.

Saengerfest Park, a small public park located on the corner of Tremont and Strand Streets on the Strand, was created in the early 1990s by the Mitchells and is now owned and managed by the Galveston Historical Foundation.

Detail view of the frontispiece of Blum Building before restoration. *Courtesy of The Tremont House.*

Blum Building before restoration showing archways closed with cinder blocks. *Courtesy of The Tremont House.*

Cynthia Mitchell died December 27, 2009, of Alzheimer's disease at the age of eighty-seven. Her funeral at Trinity Episcopal Church was attended by over five hundred people and was followed by a procession of bagpipers and mourners who walked through Galveston's streets to Tremont House, where a reception was held.

Billionaire Texas oilman, developer and philanthropist George P. Mitchell passed away at his home on July 26, 2013, at the age of ninety-four. That year, *Forbes* magazine's annual list of wealthiest Americans ranked him 239th with a net worth of $2 billion.

Twenty-Fourth Street was renamed to honor George and Cynthia Mitchell, whose efforts and generosity are largely to be credited for the revitalization of Galveston's Strand District.

# TREMONT HOUSE

## *A Rebirth*

T he transformation of the Leon & H. Blum Building and later the Belmont Hotel, into the present-day Tremont House was an immense undertaking. George Mitchell was advised by consultants that the project was too risky for shareholders of his Woodlands Corporation to be involved, so he and his wife, Cynthia, made the decision to proceed using their own money.

They hired the San Antonio firm of Ford, Powell & Carson to rehabilitate the exterior of the structure following federally mandated guidelines for historic buildings. At the same time, they were tasked with the conversion of the interior into a hotel. It would be the first major hotel in the downtown area in sixty years and named after the Tremont House in Galveston, where so much history had occurred.

Brick façades, window arches and other details of the Blum Building had been finished with stucco to resemble stone masonry. Mitchell was adamant that the restoration work be crafted in the same manner.

A fourth floor of guest rooms set behind a mansard roof with dormer windows needed to be added to the building to make the hotel operationally feasible financially. Because no photographic evidence could be found that the Blum Building had ever had a mansard-style roof, though, preservation officials would not approve the addition.

Peter Brink, director of the Galveston Historical Foundation at the time, located an etching of the architect's plan for the 1882 expansion of the building, which included the roof, but the general consensus was that it had never been built. Regardless, it provided sufficient cause for the historic commission to allow the much-needed addition, which has helped to create one of the most recognizable architectural profiles in the city today.

Milton Babbitt, president of Ford, Powell & Carson, was the architect of record and principal in charge of the project. Due to the extensive work required, he hired Michael Gaertner Sr., AIA, to be the on-site architect and remain on call twenty-four hours a day, seven days a week, locally.

Three years into his employment with the firm, both the project manager and director of construction left their firms, and Mitchell hired Gaertner to take over their duties.

"I wound up helping Mr. Mitchell with all of his projects for many years after that, for twenty-six years total," shared Gaertner. "But the Tremont House was my first project working for them—back in the days when everything was still done on paper with pencils and ink."

Crews removed the interior plaster as well as the decomposed mortar between the bricks of the structure so that it could be replaced with a stronger mixture. Before the process was completed, Hurricane Alicia arrived in August 1983.

Construction worker on the roof of the Blum Building during restoration. *Courtesy of The Tremont House.*

The storm winds drove rain into the top of the building, and the exposed bricks absorbed the water as it migrated downward over the next week. As it reached the bottom of the support columns and walls, their structure began to fail.

One of the brickmasons noticed that a column that had been completed the week prior was failing and informed Gaertner at about three o'clock one afternoon. The architect, realizing that the crews usually left the site within an hour of that time, had the word spread for all workers to remain to help stabilize them.

"We put all of the shoring towers we had inside the arched columns to relieve the load, wrapped the columns with plywood, and tied them with steel bands. But by five o'clock the cracks had opened up so much I could put my arm through the column," remembered Gaertner.

"We worked twenty-four hours a day for several weeks to try to stabilize the structure. That was a pretty exciting time. Fortunately, I didn't have any damage at my own house from Hurricane Alicia so I could be on site for the entire process."

The crew also added pipes to brace the walls to prevent any chance of a partial collapse into the street.

Walls of the Blum Building restoration project, braced after damage from Hurricane Alicia. *Courtesy of The Tremont House.*

Once the moisture problem was resolved, they rebuilt the columns with the same brick on the exterior but filled them with high-strength concrete.

With the crisis averted, reinforcing steel and tie bars were added, and interior walls were strengthened to support the weight of an air-conditioning system.

The brick exterior was then covered with the same 1800s plaster technique originally implemented to replicate masonry.

In addition to the ground-level arcade windows, many of the more than one hundred window moldings required repairs. Archival photographs were used to replicate the original detail work of the building, and the large arched bays that open onto the sidewalk were enclosed with tall glass doors.

The process of building the first floor and raising it to flood elevation held its own surprises.

When the Mitchells purchased the building, the ground floor was being used as a parking garage. Large doors that once welcomed wagons into the Blum Building provided access to cars and later to the heavy equipment used in the construction of the Tremont Hotel.

One day during construction, the front end of a tractor working on the interior grade fell into an unexpected opening in the ground.

Truck entering the ground-level parking garage of the Blum Building in the 1970s. *Courtesy of Michael Gaertner.*

"There were two great big underground cisterns that they used to capture and store rainwater," explained Gaertner. "In the downtown buildings, they built them out of brick, and they were plastered on the inside. The roof of it was made by laying down railroad ties at intervals, and they would build brick vaults in between them."

The roof of the underground vault had collapsed under the weight of the machinery, but fortunately the driver was able to gun the engine and reverse when it began to fall.

The vault, one of two eventually discovered by crews, was approximately five or six feet deep. Roofs of both cisterns were removed, and the spaces were filled with dirt to stabilize the ground.

Previous to the Mitchells' ownership, a female artist lived and worked on one of the upper floors, according to Gaertner. "She put a parachute up to kind of define her area because it was a lot of space and she just didn't like that." He added that a company that rewound electric motors was housed on the other side of an upstairs floor.

Those sorts of prior tenants did not pose a problem with the project in the emptied building, but one past tenant did. The *Galveston Tribune*, which had once operated there, had driven forklifts with immense rolls of newsprint paper on the upper floors. The weight of that process broke several beams, which needed to be addressed by Ford, Powell & Carson.

The front wooden columns of the original building were placed on brick footings but had been eaten away by termites over the years. In certain areas, there was nothing left between the footing and the column itself. Gaertner recalled that a contractor told him, "It's been there so long it just forgot how to fall down."

According to the architect, the round cornice feature at the top of the front façade was added with Clayton's amendment to Heiner's original building. Once the huge entablature was rebuilt on the ground, it was hoisted atop the hotel and emblazoned with the new Tremont House logo.

The interior brick wall, whose arched openings lead to the present-day café, was once the exterior wall of the first Blum Building before it was extended.

According to Gaertner, by the time the hotel opened Mitchell, had hired and fired three different chefs. Since every chef wants their kitchen designed in a specific way, this became a headache for construction.

"I finally got back there with a can of spray paint and a chalk line, and I laid the kitchen out myself, and I said, 'this is the way the kitchen's going to be,'" he laughed, "and that's how they built the kitchen."

Details were as important as the larger aspects of the project to the Mitchells. They insisted that the hotel would not feature keyless locks, because they believed that part of the guest experience was holding a key and turning it in the lock. They were also conscientious of the tactile design of everything from door handles to faucets.

The architect pointed out that there is a space between the original third-floor ceiling and the new floor that's under the mansard story.

Tremont House brass room keys. *Author's collection.*

"We call that the interstitial space, which means the space between stories, but it originally was like an attic." To provide extra bracing for the exterior walls, steel trussing was added in this space.

One of the most striking features of the hotel is a four-story atrium lighted by a seventy-two-foot-high gabled skylight ceiling, installed through a cut in the original frame of the building. The previous Tremont Hotel's famous atrium served as inspiration.

Bridges with bottle-green wrought-iron railings were designed to span the atrium opening and connect hallways on the second, third and fourth floors. Their custom newel caps were fabricated by Alamo Iron Works of San Antonio.

Guest rooms bordering the atrium on the upper three floors were given eleven-foot-high glazed French doors that opened onto green ironwork balconies overlooking the lobby and bar area. Their white lace curtains covered black mini blinds to provide privacy.

A Honduran mahogany–paneled glass elevator rose through the atrium, showcasing the open design, and a black marble stairway at the entrance led to the front desk, bar and café area, much as the black marble tile that lined the entrance to the earlier Tremont House had welcomed guests.

Mr. Mitchell hired General Manager Jean Pierre Picolo, formerly of the George V Hotel in Paris and the Savoy in London, to operate the Tremont House in the tradition of a European hotel. He was given a staff of ninety people to run the 120-room inn.

Meeting and event rooms, such as the Sam Houston Room and Samuel May Williams Room, were named in honor of historic figures with a connection to Tremont Hotel history.

Once the structural work was done, the interior design took place. The Mitchells hired Ann Milligan Gray of Chicago for the task. Her previous work included designs for the Ritz-Carlton in Washington, D.C., the Planter's Inn in Charleston and the Tremont Chicago Hotel. Gaertner related that she was a "four-foot six-inch firebrand with bright red hair who was a delightful person to be around."

She worked closely with Cynthia Mitchell, who had an affinity for black and white, and chose the scheme for use throughout the hotel.

It was, by coincidence, also the main color combination used in the flooring and design of the previous Tremont House.

The white-walled lobby was furnished with wicker and antiques atop black-and-white tile floors.

Three live palm trees growing through floor grates adorned the lobby, and extra lighting was installed for them. Those original palms have since died and been replaced and the additional lights removed.

Handwoven Irish wool rugs in a black and white geometric pattern were placed throughout the hotel.

A working marble fountain with a koi pond, a duplicate of one in Gray's own backyard, stood outside the café.

View of the restaurant and fountain at Tremont House opening in 1985. *Courtesy of Michael Gaertner.*

The legendary fourteen-foot rosewood Toujouse Bar was installed at the northwest end of the lobby, where it could greet guests and provide seating to enjoy occasional live music.

Cynthia Mitchell's favorite colors were continued into the guest rooms, which featured fourteen-and-a-half-foot ceilings, polished wood floors, custom woven rugs and eleven-foot-tall windows.

Brass and white enamel beds were draped with white linen eyelet coverlets, dust ruffles and pillows. The furnishings were surrounded by wallpaper with irregularly patterned black and white vertical stripes designed to be reminiscent of beadboard paneling, which extended up to the picture rails.

Architect Michael Gaertner standing at the historic Toujouse Bar in the Tremont House lobby. *Photo by author.*

Victorian reproduction armoires, marble-topped chests and gaslight-style light fixtures added to the Victorian ambiance. All of the guest room furniture was custom designed and built by Baker Furniture Company.

Guest bathrooms were adorned with one of the most expensive decorating features: tiles with a graduating black-and-white striped design hand-painted by artisans in Italy. Black marble counters and shower curtains were installed to match.

The favorite feature of many visitors, however, was the steam-heated brass towel warmers.

All of the bathrooms at the Tremont were decorated in black and white except the corner suites, where George Mitchell's preferences made an appearance. His love of geology (his minor field of study in college) led to his choice of utilizing a special marble and travertine from Italy for the countertops in those rooms, which were fabricated overseas.

Gaertner related that after the sinks were finished, "they were driven to Heathrow Airport to be shipped to Galveston. On the way there, the lorry [truck] went off the road and crashed. All of the countertops were broken, and they had to redo all of them." After a discouraging delay, they arrived and were installed in time for the hotel opening.

The Tremont project also included the construction of the Topgallant Ballroom and Wentletrap Restaurant in the Thomas Jefferson League Building behind the Blum Building, facing the Strand. A crosswalk was built to provide access from the hotel directly to these additional spaces.

The Blum Building portion of the Tremont was open as a hotel before work began on the Belmont end, which was completed in four phases according to Gaertner.

The top two floors of the old Belmont Hotel (McDonnell Building) had been unsealed so were no longer stable and had to be removed. At the time of Mitchell's purchase, it still had a corner entrance, a small painted mural above the desk area, a multicolored patterned tile lobby floor and a gilded lettered glass door to the old café. The cage elevator, derelict by that time, remained in a corner.

Pressed metal ceilings were replicated in the original pattern by the same company that had manufactured the originals and replaced.

The Belmont's original stair railing was intact, as was the atrium that opened to the second and third floors, but the balusters had been stolen. They were replicated along with the milled doors to the rooms and beadboard accents.

The Belmont's damaged floors and oak stair treads were replaced with the same varieties of wood.

Unfortunately, the cast-iron façade of the old hotel was too corroded to repair and had to be recast, which was accomplished using nineteenth-century techniques.

*Left*: View of a Tremont House guest room in 1985. *Courtesy of Michael Gaertner.*

*Right*: View of a Tremont House guest room in the Belmont wing in 1985. *Courtesy of Michael Gaertner.*

The finest suites were reserved for the Belmont side of the hotel and offered additional amenities of living areas with wet bars, jacuzzi tubs, an additional half bath and a telephone in the bathroom. The suites are served by a separate elevator.

Once the Belmont portion was completely renovated, it was connected with the Blum Building on the ground floor.

A favorite of visitors, the Tremont House's Rooftop Bar was built on top of the Belmont. It is known for providing some of the most beautiful views in town, much like the tower of the previous Tremont.

Gaertner revealed that having a bar atop the hotel was not the original plan. "This is where the pool was going to be. The pool design kept getting smaller and smaller, and eventually there was no pool at all. The weight load would have been incredible."

Tremont House Mardi Gras beads. *Author's collection.*

Before it opened to the public, it served as a sort of special retreat. "My wife and I used to go up here, and we'd be the only ones there. We'd use the telephone to order room service and have the whole place to ourselves," he recalled wistfully.

The new Tremont House opened in February 1985, just in time to enjoy the Mardi Gras festivities arranged to celebrate it. The project cost an estimated $12 million.

A simplistic iron canopy sheltered the front entrance at that time but was replaced by an aproned design emblazoned with the name a few years later.

Gaertner remembers that as guests were checking in, even the most important officers of the project, including himself, were scurrying to make sure the last details were finished including making beds as the first guests checked in. He laughs at the memory of seeing the petite Gray, listening to music on her portable audio player, quickly vacuuming an upper floor carpet.

The opening of the luxury 117-room, four-star Tremont House marked the beginning of the revitalization of downtown Galveston.

The restoration of the exterior of the Belmont wing was completed later that same year.

In 1987, a sixty-four-seat restaurant named the Merchant Prince, the nickname of the building's original owner, was added to the ground floor.

The Tremont House was refurbished throughout in 2003 at a cost of about $2 million, to ensure everything was still up to Mitchell's standards.

Toward the end of her life, Cynthia Mitchell was a victim of Alzheimer's disease. Her family asked Gaertner to replicate her home in a building in downtown Galveston to make her more comfortable during visits to the island. The architect suggested that instead, they could have her stay in her favorite suite at the Tremont, which she had designed and where she had spent so many happy hours. They adapted her favorite corner suite, which included rooms 372 and 373, for her use. Mrs. Mitchell passed away in 2009, leaving a lasting legacy in Galveston that included the Tremont House.

Hurricane Ike struck the island on September 13, 2008, flooding the ground floor of the hotel with eight feet of muddy water. Furniture and antiques were ruined, and damage was done to the Merchant Prince Restaurant, Toujouse Bar, sales offices, fitness room and several meeting rooms.

After almost nine months of repairs and renovations to protect the building from future storms, the Tremont House reopened to the public in

Candy tin in the shape of the Tremont House. *Photo by author. Item courtesy of Rosenberg Library Museum, Galveston, Texas.*

May 2009, along with a new Tremont Café. A rebirth celebration hosted by the hotel included building tours and a mini street festival.

Seven months after reopening, the hotel suffered water damage again, but this time it had nothing to do with the weather. According to the *Galveston Daily News*, an intoxicated bar patron ripped a water pipe out of a wall, causing extensive damage to the hotel kitchen, employee cafeteria and three guest rooms. As the culprit was carried out of the hotel, the charge of resisting arrest was added to his crimes.

The isolated damage was repaired in a matter of weeks.

Jeff Ossenkop, general manager of the Tremont House in 2022, oversaw a year-long, multimillion-dollar makeover of the iconic inn. The work was completed in time for the hotel's rebranding in November as part of Marriott Bonvoy's Tribute Portfolio.

Lobby furniture and décor were refreshed, and the piano moved to the center of the room for use on jazz nights. The historic Toujouse Bar still commands its position at the rear of the cocktail area.

Guest rooms were updated to incorporate contemporary designs with historically accurate hardwood floors and exposed brick walls and amenity upgrades. Penthouse units in the Quarters section of the hotel include one-bedroom lofts and two-bedroom suites.

The four historic suites in the Belmont wing, reopened as the "Mitchell Collection," are on a private floor of the hotel with a shared social space and private bar. Each suite features tin ceilings, original hardwood floors, and large living areas.

Visitors will find tributes to the Mitchells throughout the hotel.

The café was reimagined as an urban market and eatery, named Blum & Co. as an homage to the history of the building. It features a ceiling made out of a ship rope weave that opens upward to the skylight, creating airiness and intimate space at the same time.

The Rooftop Bar was updated to maximize the advantage of its 360-degree island views through glass sliding walls that can now enclose the space from the elements for year-round use. Additional seating, firepits and blankets are available to make it a welcoming retreat even in chilly weather.

Today's Tremont House is the ultimate location to stay during Mardi Gras and other island festivities as well as year-round, with downtown attractions within walking distance and gracious hospitality throughout.

The Tremont House is positioned to witness the next century of Galveston history.

# 28

# TOUJOUSE BAR

The bar at Tremont House has a colorful history all its own. The Toujouse Bar is named for Henry Toujouse, who served countless patrons across the bar over one hundred years ago and played a colorful role in Galveston's history.

Toujouse came to Galveston in 1872 from France when he was thirty years old. He evidently had either experience or a natural ability in the hospitality business, because he was swiftly hired as a bartender at the Opera House Saloon.

The saloon was on the ground floor of the five-story mansard-roofed New Galveston Theater, which opened on February 25, 1871, just months before Toujouse's arrival. Built by Willard Richardson, the theater was soon renamed the Tremont Opera House and became the most notable playhouse in the state. Visually impressive, the five story brick structure featured cast-iron street-level fronts, a mansard-style roof with galvanized iron cornices and a twenty-five-foot-wide entrance that led to the second-floor lobby.

Located on the corner of Market and Tremont Streets, the theater was immediately successful in booking well-known talent, and the saloon did a brisk business.

The saloon was owned by fellow Frenchman John M. Couget, who hired Toujouse and Arthur Michels as his assistants, though Toujouse was quickly promoted to chief bartender. He witnessed the conversations of the most famous participants of the "Golden Age" of Galveston from across his bar.

When Couget passed away in 1876, the bartenders assumed control of the establishment, renaming it Toujouse & Michels Saloon. They remained business partners until Michels retired in 1882.

That year, Toujouse renamed the bar once again, choosing the Sample Room Saloon, although locals still referred to it as the Opera House Saloon. Using the knowledge gained in the previous decade, he also branched out into importing French wines and liquors and Havana cigars—a business he would continue until he retired. A wine room and walk-in cigar storage were added at the rear of the saloon.

It was an important year in his personal life, too, as he married Mississippian Frances Susan "Sue" Blakemore, a woman eleven years his junior, on November 29, 1882. Though they never had children, the couple was known to be extremely devoted to each other.

In the following few years, as Toujouse's popularity increased, the name of the bar seemed as fluid as the drinks served there, alternately being called the Opera House Exchange Saloon, Henry's Café, Henry's Exchange or combinations thereof. Regardless of the name, business

Interior of Henry Toujouse's Saloon. *Galveston Texas History Center of the Rosenberg Library, Galveston, Texas.*

was lucrative, and he was well respected in the community. His saloon became the favored place for businessmen to gather and younger patrons to socialize.

After the 1900 Storm, he moved his business across the street and opened the Stag Hotel, which would have its own bar and provide a headquarters for his import business. The establishment also offered guests luxuries such as hot and cold artesian baths.

But when he left the former opera house, he took two things with him: the stunning fourteen-foot-long rosewood bar with hand-carved back and marble columns, and a large painting of a nude woman draped with a Texas flag that hung above it. They became the centerpieces for his palatial new saloon at the Stag, surrounded by potted palms.

As he was the region's sole agent for national brand spirits such as Old Forester, Baker's Rye Whiskey and Cascade Sour Mash, it is certain that they were the main ingredients in some of his exclusive cocktails served across the historic bar.

In 1911, he added the responsibility of being the proprietor of the New Beach Hotel, named after an ill-fated wooden structure that burned in 1898, but had given up that additional job within the year.

Toujouse sold his import business to his bookkeeper Emile Westerman in 1915 and retired with his wife to their grand Victorian home at 1702 Ball.

Sue passed away at the age of fifty-six in July 1917, after thirty-five years of marriage. Her husband never recovered from the loss. The following year, he was found wearing pajamas in his bathtub after taking his life with a gun. He left the majority of his belongings, including the home, to his nurse Myrtle McKenna.

The Stag Hotel closed shortly after Toujouse's departure, and his signature rosewood bar began a journey around the island.

In the late 1960s, a local beer parlor named the 7th Street Tavern at Seventh and Winnie Streets was a favorite hangout spot for hospital staff and students at the University of Texas Medical Branch. Also known as Judy's Place, it had been operated by proprietress Julia Gullick for about twenty-five years.

No one paid much attention to the unpolished, scarred bar where the bartenders set the orders, other than to be happy it was large and sturdy enough for the nurses to dance on. If Gullick ever knew where the bar came from, she did not mention it to anyone.

One evening in 1967, then-resident Dr. Vincent J. Privitera discovered Judy's Place was for sale and soon bought the business and furnishings. The

Interior of bar at Twenty-Third and Postoffice Streets, showing Toujouse Bar. *Galveston Texas History Center of the Rosenberg Library, Galveston, Texas.*

Toujouse Bar installed at the current-day Tremont House. *Courtesy of The Tremont House.*

purchase included the bar, tables, chairs, glassware, liquor and pictures on the wall—but not the building.

Privitera sold the business after four years and stored the bar, mirror and large painting of the nude on the upper floor of Colonel Bubbies on the Strand. He then donated the lot to the Galveston Historical Foundation.

After the bar and barback were refurbished by Joe McKay and brought back to their original beautiful appearance, they appeared in Danny Thorne's French restaurant in the Mensing Building on the Strand in 1976. Toujouse would have approved of the cuisine's connection to his heritage.

Thorne's went out of business in January 1979, and the bar was sent back into storage until it was once more refinished by McKay and placed in the atrium of the current Tremont House. At this point, the whereabouts of the painting that once hung above the bar became a mystery.

Toujouse's story has ended, but his spirit lives on (some think literally—see the following chapter on ghosts) in his beautiful bar at Tremont House along with one bit of enduring folklore. It is said that the faces at the back of the bar, feminine faces that age from left to right, represent Toujouse's enduring love for his wife throughout her life. If every good bar needs a love story, the Toujouse Bar delivers more than delicious cocktails.

# 29

# HOTEL HAUNTINGS

Every proper historic hotel has at least one ghost story.

The Tremont House located on Ship Mechanics Row is actually the third Galveston hotel to bear the Tremont name (fifth if you count smaller establishments that copied the name), but the building itself has had a long colorful history. Many believe that some who have visited the structure in the past may have never quite left and remain in spirit form.

The lobby gathering space features an exquisite rosewood bar once tended by Henry Toujouse, the barkeeper and proprietor of the Opera House Saloon in the basement of the Tremont Opera House. After the opera house closed its doors, Henry took the bar with him and opened Henry's Café at the Stag Hotel.

Henry sold his beloved bar and retired in 1915. Lost and alone after the passing of his wife and without the work that he loved, he died by suicide in his bathtub in 1918 at the age of seventy-five.

His ornately carved bar is now installed at the newest Tremont and named in his honor.

Henry may be more than just a memory though, as staff and guests have witnessed paranormal activity at the bar almost since opening day.

On Valentine's Day one year, each of the ladies on the bar waitstaff was given a long-stemmed rose by management. Gathering around the bar after closing, one of the ladies suggested they leave their roses for the bar ghost. Another waitress, scoffing at the idea of giving up her flower for a silly ghost, laid it across the corner of the bar as she retrieved her purse. An unknown force immediately sliced the bloom off the rose, leaving the startled woman with only a thorny stem.

The impish spirit of a little boy fondly called "Jimmy" by the staff plays in the kitchen, lobby, elevators and back alley of the establishment. He is rumored to be the ghost of a child who was run over by an automobile in front of the Blum Building in the 1880s. It is said that if you knock three times on the elevator doors, he will knock three times back.

Jimmy is also believed to be the cause of glasses that move by themselves across the bar, sometimes tumbling to the floor. Henry probably enjoys the company.

New employees usually experience Jimmy within a month or two, seeing the youngster out of the corner of their eye.

One woman in guest services saw a little boy playing behind a guest who was checking into the hotel. When he walked away, the boy didn't follow and seemed to disappear. When the employee later asked the guest about his son, he said he was alone and hadn't seen the child.

The most talked-about spirit at the hotel appears as a Civil War soldier in full uniform. Seen for over thirty years, he marches up and down the lobby in front of the elevators and back toward the staff offices, his ghostly clicking footsteps echoing off the marble floors. His countenance has also been seen in the bar and dining areas. Since the building itself was constructed after the Civil War, however, he must have a connection to one that stood in the same spot long ago.

On the third floor, lights and water turn on by themselves and doors open and close with no one there. One woman even claimed that "someone" grabbed her toes through the blanket as she lay in her bed at one o'clock in the morning.

Unidentified Confederate soldier. *Courtesy Library of Congress Prints and Photographs Division, Washington, D.C.*

A hotel intern from another country was gathering ice for room service when he heard a woman crying in a stairwell on the fourth floor. As he approached the sound to investigate, a strong rush of air burst past him and the sobbing stopped.

More than once, housekeeping has watched an older lady dressed in black walk out of a restroom in one of the guest rooms on the Belmont side. It seems to happen most often when they are cleaning the room, and the witnesses are sure they are alone.

The phantom of a male victim of the 1900 Storm is a bit more unnerving than his fellow ethereal residents, creating cold spots on the third and fourth floors. Especially active whenever heavy rain, lightning or windstorms occur, he attempts to alarm witnesses in order to warn of impending danger.

Roaming the hallways and visiting rooms, he turns showers, lights, televisions and ceiling fans on and off while guests attempt to sleep. The occurrences have even been known to happen in unoccupied rooms, through reports from their neighbors.

Loud claps of thunder elicit loud moans from the spirit, and a sleeping guest might hear breathing or whispering in their ear.

Following Hurricane Ike, guests on the fourth floor described being awakened by their doors being shaken and a loud pounding. The incidents were followed by the sound of one-footed stomping in the hallway accompanied by a distinct dragging noise.

One guest reported hearing someone crying for help and rapping from outside the window. That could almost be explained, except for the fact that their room was on the third floor.

The most commonly known Tremont Hotel ghost story is of Sam the salesman, who had a crippled leg and lived in the Belmont wing when it was a boarding establishment. It seems that one night, Sam's luck took a turn for the better and he won quite a bit of money on his night out. When he returned to the hotel, there was a knock on the door. He opened it to an intruder who robbed and killed him on the spot.

Guests claim to be wakened in the night with a knock on their door, and those brave enough to investigate see a ghost with an injured leg limping down the hallway. Locals believe he is still looking for his money.

Most of the ghostly reports originate from the east side of the hotel, which was originally the Belmont. More than a dozen retired seamen died in rooms there in the 1960s alone. One unfortunate fellow mysteriously fell from a window on the top floor at four in the morning.

A few rooms at the Tremont House have ghosts with their own specific habits.

Room 219's roguish entity sometimes unpacks the luggage of guests, who find the contents strewn across the floor when they wake up.

In 271, guests smell old-fashioned perfume, feel cold drafts and have an impulse to leave the room. More than once when housekeeping knocked on this door, a woman asking to be left alone responded to them. When they reported the guest to the front desk, they were informed the room was unoccupied.

A shadow figure has been seen in room 424, along with flashes of light and the water turning itself on in the middle of the night.

A presence is felt in room 474, and a burst of light can sometimes be caught on camera.

Guests at the Tremont hotel can be assured of being treated like royalty by staff and that they will never be quite alone.

# 30

# MARDI GRAS ARCHES

One of the many lasting changes native Galvestonian George P. Mitchell and his wife, Cynthia, made was to launch the revival of Mardi Gras celebrations on the island in 1985.

As part of the preparations for the festivities, the following year the couple commissioned seven well-known architects to each design a "fantasy arch" for display on the streets of the city. The project was conceived and directed by Dancie Perugini Ware.

The idea was a tribute to four temporary decorative arches that were constructed for Galveston's Saengerfest singing festival in 1881, when German immigrant choral societies from across Texas came to the city to compete. Those original arches were erected along Tremont Street at the intersections of the Strand, Mechanic, Market and Postoffice Streets.

The architects invited to participate in 1985, who donated their designs, were challenged to create fantastical interpretations of facets of Galveston's colorful history represented in an archway or gateway to span one of the island's downtown streets. Seven uniquely imaginative arches resulted from the project and cost $35,000 to $70,000 apiece to construct.

Mitchell paid for three of the arches, and real estate tycoon J.R. McConnell paid for the other four.

Tremont Street Saengerfest Arch that served as inspiration for Galveston's Mardi Gras Arches, circa 1880. *Galveston Texas History Center of the Rosenberg Library, Galveston, Texas.*

## BOONE POWELL ARCH

Positioned in front of the newly opened Tremont House on Mechanic and Twenty-Fourth Streets is the archway designed by Boone Powell, a partner in the San Antonio firm of Ford, Powell & Carson who had designed the restoration of the historic inn, as well as the 1871 Thomas Jefferson League Building behind it. It is sometimes called the Festive Arch.

The archway, which has come to symbolize Mardi Gras on the island, incorporates references to gateways and entrances to cities, the creations of nineteenth-century Galveston architect Nicholas Clayton and Galveston's status as a port city.

Constructed of plywood and festively colored open weave fabric panels on a steel tubing frame, it is internally cross-braced with steel cables for stiffening and anchored in large boxes on the sides of the street.

George Mitchell and associates at Powell Arch in front of the Tremont House. *Galveston Texas History Center of the Rosenberg Library, Galveston, Texas.*

Masts, pennants and rigging on the upper portion recall the city's past as a major seaport, and a double arch and large oculus at the top suggest Clayton's iconic designs. Sparkling Tivoli lights of purple, yellow and green outline the entire structure, brilliantly celebrating the carnival season.

The arch was designed in units so that it could be disassembled and stored for future celebrations.

Both the Powell fantasy arch and the Tremont House won design awards in the San Antonio Chapter of the American Institute of Architects 1986 Awards Program.

# CÉSAR PELLI ARCH

Angular and monochromatic, the arch conceptualized by Argentinian-born neo-modernist architect César Pelli stood at Twenty-First and Mechanic Streets. Often mistaken at first glance for a construction project in progress, its contemporary appearance was achieved with a series of layered parallel lines to form a pattern of grids. The thirty-five-foot-tall structure was described by the architect, who was the former dean of Yale School of Architecture, as incorporating four elements: wood, paint, sunlight and sky.

## CHARLES MOORE ARCH

At the intersection of Twenty-First and Postoffice Streets, Charles Moore's playful archway depicted a sort of playhouse rising above the thoroughfare, using canvas and mesh to create a canopy of waves breaking overhead. Whimsical strings of brightly colored lights and wooden stars and sea creatures made their appearances between the canvas ribbon waves. A metal moon on a mesh frame stood atop the tower.

Moore, who conceived the Piazza d'Italia for the 1984 World's Fair in New Orleans, was known as one of the most influential figures in postmodernist design.

## EUGENE AUBRY ARCH

The contemporary arch at Twenty-Second Street and the Strand created by Houstonian Eugene Aubry was undeniably the design that would be most compared to modern art. Aubrey, who worked on such iconic Houston structures as the Rothko Chapel, Glassell School of Art and Wortham Center, conceptualized the innovative effect of folds in gold pleated fiberglass curtains, topped by a colorful fish medallion. The view through the archway appropriately framed the entrance to Galveston's wharf.

## CHICAGO ARCHITECT HELMUT JAHN ARCH

Slender spire corner posts positioned at Twenty-Fifth and the Strand created a framework for German immigrant Helmut Jahn's delicate arrangement of arched rigging of red and yellow. The architect, known for his design of high-tech airports, envisioned the forty-five-foot wood and metal structure as an ode to naval masts, rigging and an upturned hull.

## Michael Graves Arch

A massive, four-legged, copper-roofed archway at the Strand and Twenty-Third Street was designed by Michael Graves. It was an instant favorite of locals and proved that "everything is bigger in Texas," sporting enormous Lone Stars on front and back.

Postmodernist Graves's other well-known projects included Disney's corporate offices in Burbank with twenty-foot-tall dwarves holding up the pediment and St. Louis's Humana Building.

## Chicagoan Stanley Tigerman Arch

Heroes of the celebrated Texas Revolution were the focus of the design fashioned by Stanley Tigerman. His weighty, four-sided Roman arch formed a thirty-four-foot cube of plywood-covered steel that featured a fractured version of Leonardo da Vinci's Vitruvian Man on the face of each side. Each corner was topped with stucco-sprayed mannequins that memorialized legendary heroes of Texas's fight for independence, bringing the height of the creation at the Strand and Twentieth Street to a towering thirty-eight feet.

Tigerman's diverse career included the designs of the Illinois Holocaust Museum and Educational Center and the Chicago Central Area plan for the 1992 Chicago World's Fair.

Law enforcement officers were stationed at the arches during parades to make sure no one climbed on them, but no arrangements were made for other days.

Media across the nation and around the world, including *Time* magazine and the *New York Times*, reported on Galveston's original fantasy arches, and exhibits were created at the Smithsonian Museum of Design and New York's Cooper-Hewitt Museum to celebrate them.

When the project was first conceived, the arches were expected to be displayed during Mardi Gras and remain up through the Texas sesquicentennial celebrations in April. But by that time, the creations spanning the downtown streets had become tourist attractions, and the issue of their removal was debated. In the following years, newspapers were peppered with stories, updates, editorials and polls reflecting opinions of whether the inconveniences they posed outweighed their beauty and draw of commerce.

In January 1986, four concrete footings had been poured directly atop the streets during construction of the Jahn arch at the Strand and Twenty-Fifth Street without notifying the city. Original plans had been for the structure to anchor on the sidewalks in front of Shearn Moody Plaza, but the architect had not taken the building's overhang into consideration, making that option impossible. The decision to move the footings into street lanes seems to have been made without proper clearances, blocking traffic lanes.

City council agreed at the end of the month to let the footings remain if surrounded by traffic barricade barrels, probably because they were still under the impression they would remain temporarily.

On May 12, two hundred dignitaries and wildflower enthusiasts, including former first lady Lady Bird Johnson, joined the Mitchells for a Hearts and Wildflowers Weekend in Galveston. The events included an Arch March taking guests on a tour of the Mardi Gras creations.

But less than one week later, the Moore Arch collapsed during a severe thunderstorm. Though the arches had been built to withstand winds up to 130 miles per hour, the crosswinds had created what amounted to microbursts, twisting the structure and causing substantial damage.

As city officials considered options concerning the rest of the arches in light of the recent loss, the Pelli Arch was disassembled and reassembled on private property at Seaside Village, 4900 Seawall Boulevard.

In late June, arch owners Mitchell and McConnell were notified they would be responsible for making sure the structures were adequately braced for Hurricane Bonnie, which thankfully later turned to the north.

August brought the removal of the troublesome Jahn Arch, which had blocked two of the four lanes of traffic, and it was put into storage.

As the remaining art pieces were removed one by one, Mitchell and McConnell, along with arch enthusiasts, regularly requested that a select few, including the Powell Arch, be allowed to stand and proposed a plan to erect one or two new arches each year. By September, however, the city council decided only the one in front of the Tremont could remain.

The Tigerman Arch was removed at the end of September and placed in storage, followed by the Aubry Ach in October. Each time an arch was disassembled, it required an additional week and a team of two men to remove the concrete footings with a jackhammer.

All but the Powell Arch continued to be removed. In 1987, its base footings were reduced in size by one inch to permit the passage of the rail trolley, which had been the only remaining objection.

When the new owner of the Seaside Village reported that the arch that had been relocated to that property did not complement the surrounding development in January 1988, the city council ordered its removal. Mitchell agreed to pay the $3,000 to dismantle it and put it in storage with the other disassembled arches.

Mitchell succeeded in raising an eighth and final arch, dubbed the Triumphal Arch, in time for Mardi Gras 1990. Designed by Aldo Rossi, it depicted four pillar lighthouses painted in unmistakable red and white stripes atop yellow bases and stood at the Strand and Twenty-Fifth Street.

First commissioned in 1986, the forty-five-foot-square, thirty-five-foot-tall structure was adorned with three regional flags hung from a truss spanning two of the giant towers. Rossi, who was known for designing Il Teatro del Mondo, a floating theater on a barge in Venice, attended the Mardi Gras celebration that year wearing a lighthouse-shaped hat to match his creation.

The Ross Arch, too, was removed, leaving the Powell Arch the only survivor at this time. Refurbished for Mardi Gras 2023, the Powell Arch sees the Grand Night Parade pass beneath each year and is a favorite photo spot for visitors and locals.

# INDEX

## A

Adams, Louis Jack and Augusta  143
Adoue, Louis A.  134
Aguillo, Jose  83
Aiken, Elmer Damron  109–112
Allen, John M.  18
Andler, F.  116
Andrews, Byron  73
Arthur, Chester A.  45
Atkins, Captain  65
Aubry, Eugene  176
Aulanier, Alphonse  135–136
Axman, John  80, 83
Ayers, J.  20
Ayers & Jacobs  20
Ayers, Theodore  40
Aziola Club  86–87

## B

Babbitt, Milton  152
Ballinger, William Pitt  73
Barclay, Delancey  61

Barclay, Nellie Jones  61
Barnard, Thomas  26
Barnes Institute  74
Bartlett, Lovell J.  81
Barton, Clara  97, 99–104
Barton, Stephen E.  101
Bates, Joseph  73
Bavoux, Jean Baptiste  137
Bayland Orphan's Home for Boys
    131, 137
Beach Hotel  52, 53
Beauclerc, Chef  48
Bedell, John Y.  109
Beers, William Francis  51
Belmont Hotel  135, 141, 144, 145,
    148, 151, 159
Bennett, Dr.  25
Birrs, George  48
Blakeman, E.  136
Blakemore, Susan  165
Blum, Alexander  73
Blum, Ben  73
Blum, Hyman  129
Blum, Joseph  129

Blum, Leon  67, 121, 128–131
Blum, Sylvain  129
Boddeker, William  48
Bonaparte, Prince Jerome Napoleon
    45
Booth, Edwin  61, 76–78
Booth, John Wilkes  76
Borwell, James Coates  108
Bowen, R.D.  116
Brink, Peter  151
Brown, James Moreau  40, 73
Brown, J.S.  73
Brusig, Theodore  139
Bryan, Guy  20
Bryan, Moses Austin  18
Burgess, Charles A.  61
Burnett, J.H.  39, 47, 113
Burnett & Kilpatrick  29, 45, 47

## C

Callaway, Reverend Jesse M.  138
Card, B.C.  73
Carr, Larry  79, 80, 82
Carter, Robert  79–80
Clayton, Nicholas J.  29, 30, 42–44,
    51, 122, 126, 155, 174
Cleveland, Charles L.  57
Cleveland, Grover  45
Cody, William  58–63
Coghlan, Charles Francis  88–91
Cohen, Rabbi Henry  44
Collins, J.P.  19
Cooke, Henry C.  139
Coombs, Mary Agnes  101
Cotton, William  19
Couget, John M.  164–166
Courtney, Emma L.  73
Crain, J. Ed  116
Crane, Stephen  84–87
Crossman & Simpson  81

Cross, Thomas  79–80
Culbertson, Robert J.  97

## D

D'Alton, Dr.  136
Davie, John P.  57
Davis, Walter  94
Delaney, John  69
Denier, Lydia  61
de Pardonnet, Baron George  50
Diaz, A.  45
DiMare, Joseph  117
Ducie, Mary Lorena  43
Dyer, Joseph Osterman  138

## E

Easton, Harry Van  93
Easton, William  55
Edison, Thomas  87, 96
Edmundson, Captain  65
Edwards, Maze  76
Egert, John  116
Eldridge, Nora  73
Electric Pavilion  43, 51
Elliott, John F.  48
Erhard, Fred E.  116, 134
Escobedo, Mariano  40
Ewalt, George  55, 56, 57, 107,
    114, 115

## F

Ferrier, A.  131
Field, Robert  18
Fielder, S.H.  61
Fields, R.M.  113
Fisher Sisters  55, 105–108, 109
Fly, Dr. Ashley W.  52, 85–86

Ford, Powell & Carson  151, 152, 155, 174
Foster, Hoskins  116
Fowler, Charles  136
Franck, Gustave B.  138
Fraser, W.A.  92
Freiberg, M.  73
French, A. Frank  73
French, James Henry  40

# G

Gaertner  117, 152, 153, 155, 157, 158, 159, 160, 161
Galloway, Rex  145
Galveston Artillery  71, 72
*Galveston Commercial Reporter*  134
*Galveston Daily News*  18, 64, 85, 114, 134, 162
Galveston Historical Foundation  134, 147
*Galveston Tribune*  102, 109, 110, 134, 155
Gammon, Dr. William  55, 56, 107, 114
Garfield, James A.  45
Garten Verein  63
Geller, Pearl, and Isadore Meyer  144
Giles, Val C.  52
Girardin House  82
Goldthwaite, Joseph Graham  40
Graber, Jimmy Lee  134
Granger, Gordon  25, 26
Grant, Ulysses S.  45, 67–75
Graves, Michael  177
Gray, Ann Milligan  157, 161
Green, Ernest  61
Grosbeck, John D.  135
Gueringer, Clarence Henry  52, 53, 54
Gullick, Julia  166

# H

Haden, Dr. John M.  73
Halff, Felix  40
Harrison, Benjamin  45
Harrod, B.A.  126
Harvey, J.H.  39, 61
Hawley, Robert Bradley  97
Hayes, Rutherford B.  19, 20, 45
Heiner, Eugene T.  121, 125–127
Henderson, J. Pinckney  18
Hill, George A.  116
Hoecker, Oscar R.  116
Hogg, James Stephen  45
Hotel Galvez  56
*Houston Chronicle*  114
Houston, Sam  17, 21, 22–24, 84
*Houston Telegraph*  19
Hughes, W.E.  53, 83
Hunt, Memucan  18
Hurricane Alicia  152, 153
Hurricane Ike  161, 171

# I

Isenhour, Viola  125

# J

Jahn, Helmut  176
Jean Laffite Hotel  57
John, Noah Noble  40
Johnson, Lady Bird  178
Johnson, Samuel  82
Jones, Anderson  81
Jones, Anson  18
Jones, Starr S.  50
Jordan, Dave  65
Julie (enslaved woman)  136

# K

Kempner, Harris  40, 48
Kilpatrick, R.J.  39, 47, 113
Knights of Momus  64–66
Kopperl, B.J.  138
Kopperl, Herman Benjamin  138, 142
Kopperl, Isabella Dyer  138
Kopperl, Moritz  40, 73, 142
Kopperl, Sara Ann  139
Korst, George  54–55, 95
Kuntz, Clara  81

# L

Labatt, Henry Jacob  73
Ladies of the Dominion  66
Lamar, H.J.  45
Law, Charles  96–97
Lemcke, Fred D.  116
Leonard, Charles H.  11, 50, 70, 72, 73
Levy Brothers  89
Levy, Henrietta  129
Lincoln Guards  72
Lone Star Band  39, 65, 72
Lubbock, Francis R.  24
Lynch, Michael  29, 30
Lyons, John R.  19

# M

Maddern, Richard  39, 40
Malone, James Lewis  54
Mandich, George  117
Mansfield, Colonel  70
Martin, Edward  61
Marx, Louis  82
Marx, Marx  40, 48, 57
Mayo, Ernest  97
McCarthy, Alex  61

McConnell, J.R.  173, 178
McDonnell, Bernard J.  136, 137
McDonnell, Francis  137
McDonnell, Winifred  136
McGinley, George  48, 83, 113
McKay, Joe  168
McKenna, Myrtle  166
McKenzie, Donald N.  138
Menard, Michel B.  64
Mercer, Dr. William  102
Michels, Arthur  164–165
Miller, Clara  81
Milner Hotel  135, 144
Mistrot Brothers  132–134
Mistrot, F.E.  61
Mitchell, Cynthia Woods  146–150, 157, 161
Mitchell, Ernest Carroll  144
Mitchell, George P.  145, 146–150, 151, 152, 154, 155, 156, 158, 173, 178
Montgomery, Rose  81
Moody, William Lewis  52, 73
Moore, Charles  176
Moore, Dr. John R.  116
Moore, James  48, 54
Morlacchi, Giuseppina  58, 60
Moser, James Henry  84
Mott, Marcus  40, 65, 70
Murdoch's Bathhouse  109
Murray, O.G.  73
Mussey, Ellen Spencer  102

# N

Neil, Denis  25, 138
New Tremont Hotel  135, 142
1900 Storm  43, 54, 55, 56, 90, 92–98, 103, 106, 112, 133, 166, 171
Norwood, Nathaniel  15–17

# O

O'Hanlon, Mr. 48
Omohundro, John Baker "Texas Jack" 58, 60, 62
Opera House Saloon 164, 165, 169
Ord, Edward Otho Cresap 70
Ossenkop, Jeff 162
Ousley, Clarence 85

# P

Palmetto House 135–137
Pavlova, Anna 45
Peck, Arthur L. 134
Peck, Dolores A. 134
Pelli, César 175–176, 178
Penland, Samuel Moore 84, 85, 87
Perry, Eliza 19
Picolo, Jean Pierre 156
Pitou, Gertrude Coghlan 90
Powell, Boone 174–175
Pratt, H.C. 73
Privitera, Dr. Vincent J. 166, 168

# R

Reagan, John Henninger 40
Red Cross 97, 99, 101, 102
Rhodes, H.W. 52
Richardson, Willard 164
Rising Sons of Progress 72
Roberts, Elizabeth 97
Roberts, Oran Milo 50
Rossi, Aldo 179
Royal Hotel (Hotel Royal) 135, 138–142

Ruhl, William 81
Runge, Julius 40, 73

# S

San Jacinto House 135–136
Santa Fe Castle (Pignataro Castle) 117
Sayers, Joseph Draper 54, 97, 101
Sayles, Henry 57
Sbisa, Bernard 46–47
Schmitz, Frank W. 139
Seabock, Erle 114
Sealy, George 40, 73
Sealy, John 100, 102
Seeligson, Henry 40
Shaw, Joshua Clark 19, 20
Sheppard, Morris 92
Sheridan, Francis C. 16, 17
Sheridan, Philip 69, 73
Sinclair, William H. 74
Sisters of the Mysterious Ten 72
Skinner, J.D. 40
Sloan, H.T. 73
Smith, Cleofas F. 53
Smith, Dr. Ashbel 70, 73
Smith, Fred 81
Smith, P.A. 144
Solms-Braunfels, Prince Carl of 18
Sommers, Richard 48
Sons of Jerusalem 72
Spann, Justice 82
Spencer, Frank M. 97, 101
Star Drug Store 43, 61
Steger, Emile E. 57
Stevens, Elizabeth 138
Stevens, Frank W. 61
Steward, Fred S. 29
Stewart, E.R. 138
Stirling Hotel 135, 142–143

Stirling, John Joseph 139, 142–144
Stone, H.C. 57
Sullivan, Morris 81, 83
Sweeny, Captain 65

# T

Texas A&M 46–47, 126, 146, 147
Texas State Volunteer Guard 101
Thompson, Sandy 139
Thompson, T.C. 138
Thorne, Danny 168
Tigerman, Stanley 177
Toujouse, Henry 164–169
Trueheart, H.M. 43
Turner, Lucy 81

# U

United Brothers of Friendship 72

# V

Vanderbilt, William H. 45
Vautrin, Ruth K. 143
Vidor, Charles 57, 73
Vrydaugh, J.A. 125

# W

Waldin, R. 82
Ward, Fred L. 101
Ware, Dancie Perugini 173
Warren, Margaret Etta 112
Washington Guards 19, 57, 65,
    71, 72
Weaver, Henry 79
Welch, Dr. S.M. 52
Wenzel, C.C. 139
Westerlage, R.H. 139

Westerman, Emile 166
Whales, Willie 74
Wheeler, William A. 45
Wickliff, Charles A. 18
Wilde, Oscar 51
Williams, Henry Howell 15
Williams, Sam J. 116
Winters, Julia 81
Wirtz, Charles 48
Wright, Horatio 26

# Z

Ziegler, Charles 116
Ziegler, Jesse A. 116
Zouaves 20–21

# ABOUT THE AUTHOR

*G*alveston's *Tremont House Hotel* is Kathleen Maca's fifth book about unique aspects of Galveston's past. She enjoys writing about history and folklore and especially uncovering the little-known and surprising stories from the past that prove that history can be as fascinating as any fiction.

A graduate of Sam Houston State University, she is focusing her energies on research and writing after a full career in the field of advertising. She and her work have garnered attention on statewide and national television, radio shows, podcasts and in magazines.

She also drives across the Lone Star State for her travel blog *Tales from Texas* at kathleenmaca.com.

A member of the Association for Gravestone Studies, she is also a cemetery historian, cemetery restorationist, Certified Tourism Ambassador, genealogist, admiral in the Texas Navy and a member of the Sam Houston Chapter of the NSDAR and the Bay Area Genealogy Society.

Her other books include *Galveston's Broadway Cemeteries*, *Ghosts of Galveston*, *Ghostly Tales of Galveston* and *A History of the Hotel Galvez*.

Additionally, Kathleen provides presentations, historic neighborhood tours, cemetery tours and ghost tours on Galveston Island, which can be found on her website.